Scientific Properties and
Occult Aspects of

Twenty-Two Gems, Stones, and Metals

A Comparative Study Based on
the Edgar Cayce Readings

ASSOCIATION FOR
RESEARCH AND
ENLIGHTENMENT

Revised Edition

A.R.E. PRESS • VIRGINIA BEACH • VIRGINIA

REVISED EDITION

ISBN 87604-110-1

The following articles are reprinted by permission
from *The A.R.E. Journal:*
"Reflections of a Rockhound" © 1973 by the Association
for Research and Enlightenment, Inc.
"The Stones of Egypt" © 1974 by the Association
for Research and Enlightenment, Inc.
"Lapis Lazuli" © 1975 by the Association for Research
and Enlightenment, Inc.

15th Printing, November 1998

Printed in the U.S.A.

CONTENTS

THE PHILOSOPHY OF
THE EDGAR CAYCE READINGS

When discussing the areas of psychic experience approached by means of gem vibrations, astrology, numerology, hypnosis, automatic writing, etc., the Cayce discourses insisted that these were not psychic "toys," but tools which, if used correctly, could be extremely helpful in spiritual development. If abused or used for selfish purposes, they could "turn and rend" the user.

Thus, in studying readings on the occult influences of gems, stones and metals,* with the object of putting the information to personal use, the reader should have a general idea of the philosophical background of the psychic discourses.

The philosophy of the readings is often described as universal. That is, it is not at odds with any major philosophy or religion and, in its structure, contains elements of various schools of thought. It combines and reconciles the mysticism and introspection of the East with the social consciousness and evangelism of Western Christianity. From the purely religious standpoint, Jesus the Christ is its apex.

Human life, the readings assert, is a temporary phase of the eternal life of the soul—experienced by choice or necessity for the purpose of gaining understanding and progress toward the perfection required for full reunion with God. Through series of experiences in various planes of consciousness, including the Earth, the soul is said to become aware of and obedient to Divine law.

The readings encourage an individual search for both *understanding* and *application* of spiritual law, repeatedly paraphrasing Saint James' epistle with the warning, "Knowledge not lived is sin!" An immediate goal of such searching would be the solution of all the practical problems of life—spiritual law being superior to all physical laws.

Meditation and prayer, combined with creative *action*—or, in other words, translated into service—are asserted to be the keys to understanding and the power resulting from it. The reader

---

*Psychic influences of color, music, dancing, flowers, etc., are also discussed in the readings, but are not covered in this study.

will notice that the vibrations of certain semi-precious stones are said to be aids in the practice of meditation. Other gems, stones, and metals are pointed out as having highly individualized effects—both spiritual and physical—for persons who can discover and use the type best suited to their own electrodynamic character.

The object of this study is not to recommend any particular gem or stone for an individual. Rather, it presents the criteria to be found in the Cayce readings by which an individual can investigate, test and, perhaps, choose that which is most beneficial in his own case.

PART I
OCCULT PROPERTIES AND USES OF GEMS, STONES, AND METALS

Magical or occult knowledge is knowledge based upon senses which surpass our five senses and upon a capacity for thinking which surpasses ordinary thinking, *but it is knowledge translated into ordinary logical language, if that is possible or insofar as it is possible.*

Ouspensky (1956, p. 16)

The belief in the magical properties of stones and gems is, indeed, of immemorial antiquity; a cuneiform inscription gives a list of stones facilitating conception and birth and including love and hatred . . . With the Magdalenian skeleton found at Duruthy was discovered a necklace of fifty canine teeth, three of lion and the rest of bear, most of them ornamented in some fashion: one with the figure of a seal, and one with that of a pike.

Evans (1922, p. 13)

Introduction

The employment of gems, stones, and metals for influencing a variety of physical, mental, and spiritual conditions in man was once an exact and highly developed science. This science is at present greatly corrupted from its former state, and at a very low level. It is the purpose of this study to present "new" knowledge (new to our time) on the occult properties of gems, stones, and metals—knowledge that was obtained psychically through Edgar Cayce from what the readings termed the "universal consciousness." The importance that this branch of knowledge has had in the past and the benefits that can be derived from its study in the present are indicated in the following passages from the readings:

Q-5. *What should my hobby be?*
A-5. The gathering of data of the nature that is unusual, respecting the jewels of all characters; how that some have

played such a part in the love affairs, in the life and death, and in the home and in the empire building of some lands. Few realize how much part some of these have played in this land, or in England, or in France, or in Persia, India, Hindustan, and the crown jewels in Russia. All of these, and the data of same, would be a lovely hobby—and bring those vibrations good for the body.   2522-1, F. 19
                                              born 4/8/22

Q-12. Why were these stones mentioned to me in the beginning?
A-12. They are as those things of old, which if followed ... may be used as stepping-stones for the understanding of vibrations as related to the mineral forces and as to man.
                                              440-18, M. 24
                                              born 4/24/10

Mechanism of Influence

There are no modern-day scientific theories that treat the mechanism by which gems, stones, and metals transmit influences to human beings. Many of us, however, would like to know more about the phenomenon. A very few of our number appear to have actually apprehended the underlying truths: consider, for instance, the words of the great yogi, Paramahansa Yogananda (1956, p. 242):

> Pearls and other jewels as well as metals and plants, applied directly to the human skin, exercise an electromagnetic influence over the physical cells. Man's body contains carbon and various metallic elements that are present also in plants, metals, and jewels. The discoveries of the rishis in these fields will doubtless receive confirmation some day from physiologists. Man's sensitive body, with its electrical life currents, is a center of many mysteries as yet unexplored.

Edgar Cayce shed some light upon this mechanism of "electromagnetic influence" in a few of the readings that he gave. In one, given for a person with latent psychic abilities, we find:

Q-9. You will examine the [lapis] stones which I hold, telling which is the most powerful for the various uses it may be used for. You will explain these various uses and recommend those that would be most helpful.
A-9. In giving that which may be helpful it is necessary, for this mind or body seeking same, that there be [given] rather

2

the analysis of the composition of the stones as related to their vibrations—as relate then to a human body, see?

Either of these shows a variation of their composition; as to the elements of those influences that make for vibrations in the ether as related to that which may be effective in drawing to or disseminating from—through, of course, the vibrations being . . . of the positive and negative natures in the very stone itself—making for, then, the analysis: knowing same by what is called the constituents of it, through the mineralogy, the activity through those channels themselves. We would then find that the one that is the nearer in accord to the vibrations of the body that may use same would be the more effective with *that* particular body. Yet the very *nature* of the thing [stone] makes it effective with any—*any*—human body, you see; but the more effective with one that is more in accord, or whose positive and negative vibrations are according with the stone itself, see? for it [the stone] throws off as well as draws in . . . through the positive-negative vibration. This assists, then, in the unison as a relationship. This is as a comparison—don't confuse it and say it is electricity; it [the relationship] is electrical, of course, in its vibration, but as the stone in its vibration is then in sympathy with a body that is also sympathetic—or may be said to be *sensitive*—it [the stone] assists in "stepping up" the sensitiveness of the body as would the electrical vibration in an alternating force step up by the addition of . . . forces of electrical vibration being thrown off from other channels in making it more powerful. See? [Step up] Towards what? Towards the effectiveness in its sensitiveness (that is, the body) as to what it may be seeking. Hence, as given of old, use such for the abilities to become [grow towards] more of all those influences called in the present psychic, clairaudient, or any of those vibrations that build up or "step up" a body. [Such vibrations are] Also effective, of course, in bringing to the body the abilities to become more effective in giving out of itself for activity in any of these various directions.   440-18, M. 24
                                                                                             born 4/24/10

Another reading states:

. . . the very elements of body—through which spirit and mind manifest—are atomic in their nature. Hence so are the elements of this stone indicated, that partakes of most of the elements that are to man of great influence or power, because of their representation in the body.

Hence the radical activity of radium, as well as the strengthening influences of gold, the stabilizing influence of silver, are all a part of those elements that make for the transmission through the activity of the very vibratory forces themselves . . .   1931-1, M. 20
                                                                                             born 9/11/19

3

Stones and Metals for Attunement

Vibratory forces arising from certain stones and metals collaborate with similar forces originating within individuals to permit them to attune to the Creative Forces of the universe. In this way men may receive and transmit healing vibrations, spiritualize their desires, or obtain "food" for soul development, to mention a few possibilities. The following reading excerpts illustrate this point:

[It is] Well that the entity have the stones or minerals about self when in periods of meditation, or in those periods when it may find itself the more easily attuned to the influences that may use the body, either in the healing forces that flow through—through its attunements, or through the visions and the associations of the entity; [have] the chrysolite or the amethyst. For the color purple should be close to the body; and the perfumes or odors as of lavender have their influence—not as in great quantity, but [in] that [quantity] which makes for attunements.

688-2, F. 61
born 6/23/1873

Q-7. If I were to wear the stone, as suggested in a previous reading, would it improve my mental, physical or spiritual condition?
A-7. This naturally is to make, as indicated, the body more sensitive to the higher vibrations. Not so much in the physical health as in the mental and spiritual influences, that would be materially aided.

691-2, F. 34
born 4/11/1900

Stones and Metals for Protection

Adverse influences upon the normal functions of our bodies, minds, or souls (?) can be counteracted, in some instances, by the wearing of certain gems, stones, or metals. Yogananda (1956, p. 171) cites an instance in which his master, Sri Yukteswar, recommended that Yogananda wear an armlet of silver and lead (for impending liver trouble). These are Sri Yukteswar's words:

Just as a house may be fitted with a copper rod to absorb the shock of lightning, so the bodily temple can be protected in certain ways.

Electrical and magnetic radiations are ceaselessly circulating in the universe; they affect man's body for good and ill. Ages ago our rishis pondered the problem of combating the adverse effects of subtle cosmic influences. The sages discovered that pure metals emit an astral light which is powerfully counteractive to negative pulls of the planets. Certain plant combinations were also found to be helpful. Most effective of all are faultless jewels of not less than two carats.

The practical preventive uses of astrology have seldom been seriously studied outside of India. One little-known fact is that the proper jewels, metals, and plant preparations are valueless unless the required weight is secured and unless the remedial agent is worn next to the skin . . .

For general purposes I counsel the use of an armlet made of gold, silver, and copper. But for a specific purpose I want you to get one of silver and lead.

A few of the Cayce readings recommend metals or stones as protective devices:

Do not take this as being something of superstition, or as something that would be a good luck charm—but if the entity will wear about its person, or in its pocket, a metal that is carbon steel—preferably in the groin pocket—it will prevent, it will ionize the body—from its very vibrations—to resist cold, congestion, and those inclinations for disturbance with the mucous membranes of the throat and nasal passages.

1842-1, M. 32
born 7/31/07

The lapis lazuli, worn close to the body would be well for the general health of the body—and this you will have to be careful of very soon.   **3416-1, F. 40**
born 1/15/04

. . . the lapis ligurius would bring much that will act in that manner as would be termed a *protective* influence, if kept about the entity.   **1931-1, M. 20**
born 9/11/19

. . . the beryl and scarab should be a portion of the entity's dress, *ever;* either worn as the amulet, the ring, or such, will make for a safety in the entity's present experience.

1719-1, M. 10
born 6/19/20

Stones Used for Destruction

Just as it is desirable for us to be aware of the different uses to which atomic energy can be put, so it is well for us to realize that there are destructive, as well as constructive, uses for gems, stones, and metals. The following reading describes an instance in which misuse of the forces transmitted through a single stone adversely affected an entire civilization:

Q-1. Going back to the Atlantean incarnation—what was the Tuaoi stone? Of what shape or form was it?

A-1. It was in the form of a six-sided figure, in which the light appeared as the means of communication between infinity and the finite; or the means whereby there were the communications with those forces from the outside. Later this came to mean that from which the energies radiated, as of the center from which there were the radial activities guiding the various forms of transition or travel through those periods of activity of the Atlanteans.

It was set as a crystal, though in quite a different form from that used there. Do not confuse these two, then, for there were many generations of difference. It was in those periods when there was the directing of aeroplanes, or means of travel; though these in that time would travel in the air, or on the water, or under the water, just the same. Yet the force from which these were directed was in this central power station, or Tuaoi stone; which was as the beam upon which it acted.

In the beginning it was the source from which there was the spiritual and mental contact.

Understand, these are the following of laws—if there would be the understanding or comprehension of these. For, as has been given, the basis, the beginning of law carries all the way through. And that which comes or begins first is conceived in spirit, grows in the mental, manifests in the material; as was this central force in the Atlantean experience. First it was the means and source or manner by which the powers that be made the centralization for making known to the children of men, and children of God, the directing forces or powers. Man eventually turned this into that channel for destructive forces—and it is growing towards this in the present.

2072-10, F. 32
born 3/25/10

The destructive use of energy transmitted through stones in prehistoric times is described in several other readings, including the following:

Q-29. What is the best substance for induction, conduction, transmission of etheronic energy?

A-29. This is as raised power that would be produced from a combination of crystals. This should be rather interesting to this body, for it is very much like that used by the body in destructive forces in the Atlantean sojourn! Not that which caused the cosmic ray, or the death ray, or the healing ray—but the ray that came from setting of the prismatic influences from high heating—it may be from Arcturus or it may be from the

sun; though Arcturus would be nearer proper. The sun may be induced to make for destructive or constructive forces, either one. 440-3, M. 23
born 4/24/10

Another reading points out that it is possible intentionally or unintentionally to transmit destructive influences to others by means of certain gems:

... those [types of lapis linguis] that are of the greater value as the touchstones or those that may receive (we are putting it in another form or manner) a blessing and transmit same to another, or a curse and transmit same to another, will be found in the nature where the greater portion of the azurite is evidenced in the immediate vicinity. 440-11, M. 23
born 4/24/10

The Intended Uses
Of Occult Properties of Gems, Stones, & Metals

The following two reading excerpts are typical of the central theme developed in the readings on gems, metals, and stones. They stress the uses of these substances for engendering helpful vibrations in the experience of the wearer and for attuning oneself to the Creative Forces of the universe.

For, as is understood by the entity, all creation is a manifestation of that creative influence or force called God; and these elements [in stones] bring such to this body, for they are a part of the evolution of vibration—as may be seen from the entity's development through the earthly sojourns as well as through the astrological sojourns that have been a part of the entity's experience ...
Thus, as these elements are a part of its creations, so may they bring those helpful vibrations about the entity. Not merely as an omen; for each soul is a part of the whole creation, and gives off that help, or that urge which is latent and manifested in the relationships with others. So may these elements bring helpful environs, helpful forces in the experience of the entity. 2282-1, F. 64
born 3/8/1876

Q-2. How can I use the ... vibrations from metal, from stones, which influence me, to advantage in my present life?
A-2. As these are but lights, but signs in thine experience, they are as but a candle that one stumbles not in the dark. But worship *not* the light of the candle; rather [worship] that to which it may guide thee in thy service. So, whether [thou art guided by] the vibrations of numbers, of metals, of stones, these are merely to become the necessary influences to make

7

thee in attune, one with the Creative Forces; just as the pitch of a song of praise is not the song nor the message therein, but is a helpmeet for those that would find strength in the service of the Lord. So, use them to attune self. How, ye ask? As ye apply, ye are given the next step.

Q-3. Should I carry these stones on my person? and how may I know through meditation the message they would give me?

A-3. [Carry on person] If necessary. And how may ye know? These do not give the messages! They only attune self that the Christ Consciousness may give the message! Listen to no message of a stone, of a number, even of a star; for they are but servants of the Lord and Master of all—even as thou!

707-2, M. 58
born 11/2/1876

We might infer from the last of these two readings that the ultimate function of gems, stones, and metals in our lives is *to aid us in finding the Christ Way.*

PART II
GEMS, STONES, AND METALS OF THE READINGS

Introduction

Each of the descriptions of gems, stones, or metals that follows is made up, wherever practicable, of three parts. The first part consists of an introductory paragraph that reviews the known scientific features of each material—features such as the precise mineral name (given in italics), color and appearance, hardness, chemical composition and occurrence in nature. A second part is made up of one or two paragraphs that relate some of the lore that surrounds each of the various substances. The third part of each description is composed of excerpts from the readings.

Dana's Textbook of Mineralogy (Dana and Ford, 1951) has been consulted frequently for the physical and chemical properties of the various stones. Hardness values that are given for the stones correspond to those of the Mohs hardness scale:

Hardness Value	Representative Mineral	Simple Tests
1	Talc	Feels greasy to touch of hand
2	Gypsum	Easily scratched by fingernail
3	Calcite	Cut readily by knife
4	Fluorite	Scratched easily by knife
5	Apatite	Scratched by knife with difficulty
6	Orthoclase	Barely scratched by knife; will scratch common glass; can be filed
7	Quartz	Little touched by file
8	Topaz	Cannot scratch corundum
9	Corundum	Will scratch topaz
10	Diamond	Hardest substance; cannot be scratched by any other mineral

Information on the "magic" and lore of gems and stones has been taken largely from two well-known works, *The Curious Lore of Precious Stones,* by Kunz (1913), and *The Magic and Science of Jewels and Stones,* by Kozminsky (1922). The legends and magical accounts that are cited are good examples of the quality of information that is commonly available to people interested in the influences of different gems and stones. Additional studies of the legends and "ancient" history of gems are cited in the bibliography.

1. AGATE

Agate is a variegated *chalcedony;* that is, a variety of cryptocrystalline quartz. The colors of this stone are displayed in bands or irregular "cloudlike" forms. "The bands are the edges of layers of deposition, the agate having been formed by a deposit of silica from solutions intermittently supplied, in irregular cavities in rocks, and deriving the concentric waving courses from the irregularities of the walls of the cavity." (Dana and Ford, p. 473) Agate has a hardness of 7 and its chemical formula is SiO_2. It is named after the river Achates, in Sicily, where the first specimens were reported to have been found, according to the Greek scientist Theophrastus. It is found in many places throughout the world, but the best specimens are found in India, Brazil, Uruguay, and the Rhineland, Germany.

The agate is generally believed to have been the eighth stone in the breastplate of the High Priest, and it was held in great respect by ancient scholars who saw in certain specimens of it the symbolical third eye. More recently, Swedenborg saw in the agate the symbol of the spiritual love of good. Many legends concerning its healing properties are related by Kozminsky and Kunz; some of its uses being to banish fear, to protect children against epilepsy, and to harden tender gums.

Reading Excerpts

As to the astrological aspects, as we find, these are of specific activity. The omen the body should ever wear on the person is a Maltese cross, or a stone of the agate or amethyst—for their vibrations are the better. But, as the body should comprehend in regard to all such influences, it is as to what the body does about same; not that it relies upon such [influences], but knowing that such influences aid in increasing the ability or efficiency in the periods of exertion or activity, use them rather as stepping-stones and not those things upon which the activities in a mental and spiritual plane would be builded. They are stepstones rather than foundations, then, in the experience.
                                                      500-1, F. 35
                                                  born 7/26/1898

The astronomical, the numerological, the environs of the creations in the vibrations from metals, from stones, from those of every form, have—through the experience of the entity—at times had their influence; and thus bear for the entity something that must be used as an omen, or as an experience that may aid the entity in making the proper interpretations of those things that to many an one are not lawful to be spoken in materiality—hence come only to those who have eyes to see, through the spiritual realms, or who have ears to hear the music of the spheres, the growing or the beauty in all the relationships to man that make for expressions of the divine that may be, and is, a portion of man's experience.

No man, no physical matter, has ever seen *God* at any time; only the *manifestations* of Him.

... For to whom much is given in any manifested form, of him much is required. For *these,* as we find, my son, are as the basic, elemental principles of truth itself. It is a growing thing, even as the knowledge of God, even as the knowledge of truth, even as the knowledge of life; which all are words, yet mean the variations of expressions of that *ye,* my son, would worship as a living God.

Hence we find the agate, the beryl, should be *stones* with the vibrations and under the influence that the entity may find carrying an incense to the finer self that makes for an awakening, an opening of the inner self for the *receptiveness.* And attunement is made through such vibrations, just as there may be with the tungsten in a portion of a vacuum that may raise those sound waves that through their relativity of activity of the electrical vibration that makes for the activity of the atomic forces in same give that which is gathered from the ether waves. So may numbers and those vibrations from stones as given, with metals such as come in the lapis lazuli, make for the raising of the attunement in self through meditation. But know these, my child, are but means—and are *not* the God-Force, *not* the Spirit, but the *manifestations* of same. 707-1, M. 58
born 11/2/1876

2. AMETHYST

Amethyst is clear *quartz,* of purple to bluish violet color. Its hardness is 7, and chemical formula is SiO_2, with perhaps a trace of manganese giving it the purplish coloration. Amethyst crystals are found in Austria, Czechoslovakia, and Rumania. In the United States, amethyst is found at Amherst, Virginia, and in North Carolina in Alexander and Lincoln counties. It is also found in Yellowstone Park, Wyoming, and in the Thunder Bay district in Ontario.

Most authorities have identified the amethyst with the ninth stone of the High Priest's breastplate. Ancient sages connected it with the ninth celestial mansion (Sagittarius) and it was the seventh precious stone which the sage Iachus gave to Appolonius of Tyana as an emblem of piety and dignity. " . . . The Rosicrucians . . . saw in the amethyst and the amethystine color a symbol of the divine male sacrifice, since the stone and the color were typical of love, truth, passion, suffering, and hope." (Kunz, p. 269)

Reading Excerpts

Again we would refer to the records as written here, regarding omens:

Amethyst stones should ever be a portion about the body, either in amulets or adornments about the body. These in their very vibration will make for an influence that has to do with the entity in its innate and manifested expressions in its associations.

1035-1, F. 18
born 4/27/17

In the choice of stones, do wear the amethyst as a pendant about the neck, as part of the jewelry. This will also work with the colors to control temperament.

3806-1, F. 15
born 6/1/29

See readings 500-1 (p. 10) and 688-2 (p. 4).

3. BERYL

Ordinary *beryl* occurs generally in hexagonal prisms, often coarse; and green is the usual color. Beryl exhibits a vitreous, but sometimes resinous, luster and may occur in yellow, green, blue, and white shades. Its hardness is 7.5 to 8 and it has the following chemical composition: $Be_3Al_2(SiO_3)_6$. This mineral is widely distributed and a few of the better-known localities in the United States are: Albany, Maine (where an 18-foot crystal was found); Grafton, New Hampshire; Chester, Pennsylvania; Stony Point, North Carolina; and Cahuilla, California.

Although the tenth stone of the breastplate may well have been beryl, some students claim that it was yellow jasper, chrysolite, or serpentine. An amulet of aquamarine beryl was believed by some ancients to banish fear, while in the Middle Ages it was thought that beryl would render the wearer unconquerable, quicken his intellect, and cure him of laziness.

Reading Excerpt

In the one before this we find [the entity] in that land known as the Egyptian. The entity [was] then in the household of the priest, and of those that waited on the companion of the priest.

In the name Is-Eli. In this experience the entity rose to power, position, place, fame, through the experiences in that period, as related to the various manners of expression of praise in music, in art, and *especially* in that of placing of stones. In the present, the innate desire to feel precious stones, to compare same, to watch the change in the color in same, is seen from this experience. These [stones] will make for much *judgment* to the entity, and the beryl and scarab should be a portion of the entity's dress, *ever;* either worn as the amulet, the ring, or such, will make for a safety in the entity's present experience. 1719-1, M. 10
born 6/19/20

See reading 707-1 (p. 11).

4. BLOODSTONE
(Heliotrope)

Bloodstone, or heliotrope, is massive *quartz,* of the variety *plasma,* but with small spots of red jasper that resemble drops of blood. Plasma is "rather bright green to leek green, and also sometimes nearly emerald green, and subtranslucent or feebly translucent." (Dana and Ford, p. 473) Its hardness is 7, and composition almost entirely SiO_2. In ancient times the bloodstone was found in quantities near Heliopolis, Egypt.

The bloodstone was believed capable of checking hemorrhages in ancient and medieval times. It was also believed to have the power to cause tempests.

Reading Excerpts

Q-14. What is the meaning of my aura, blue to purple?
A-14. As the color or tone indicates, the blue in purity and the purple towards spirituality.
Q-17. What precious stone sends out the most healing vibrations for my body?
A-17. Those of the pearl and of the bloodstone.

275-31, F. 20
born 1/17/13

Do not lay aside the rosary! Have about the entity stones that are red; as the bloodstone, the ruby, or everything of that nature—in stone but *not* in hangings or draperies.

1616-1, F. 44
born 3/6/1894

Hence we find these as signs or omens—as also the numerological, the vibratory forces of color, or those of the mineral as may be crystallized in material forces.

Hence the bloodstone or the ruby is well to ever be about the entity, upon its body; so that the very vibratory forces of same give—with that of thought in constructive forces—creative environs or vibrations for the entity in its use or application.

1770-2 F. 49
born 3/21/1889

As to stones—the bloodstone, to be sure, is that which will bring more harmony as to vibrations, but in all it is the mental in self that must bring harmony—whether the entity applies itself in music or in art.

3407-1, F. 40
born 3/21/03

Of these, then, take note: In any form, which will be seen from the sojourns in the earth, which has to do with color, as in decoration, as in wallpaper designing, as in wallboard designing, might the entity bring a great deal of joy, of harmony into the experience of those with whom he might work, or [he might] direct such [work], as a collector of stones that are colored, especially opals, emeralds, moonstone, bloodstone, what may be termed the semi-precious stones.

These not merely as a collector, but as one who might prepare or gather such for not merely setting, for each of these have their value in the effect, the vibrations that they each bring about the body.

5294-1, M. 61
born 7/23/1883

When there is the analyzing of those influences about the entity, we find that . . . the influences especially as relating to stones and the activity and vibrations arising from same would be beneficial for the entity in its application of self towards whatever activity may be chosen. Hence we would wear especially the bloodstone, cut in the form of a triangle, though ovaled on its edges. This about the body brings that vibration which will be beneficial; not merely as a "good luck" charm, not merely as something upon which to depend, but as an influence, a vibration about the entity.

For, each soul, each entity, has within its inner being the sum of what it has done, is doing, about its relationships to the whole. And this is the stone to which the entity vibrates. Thus it is a helpful force physically, an encouragement to the mental, and vibrates upon the real or inner self.

2163-1, F. 28
born 3/10/12

Keep the bloodstone close to thy body, as combined with the lapis lazuli. This if encased and worn upon the breast would bring healing, and decisions for the entity, because of the very vibrations that such create in their activity.

2282-1, F. 64
born 3/8/1876

14

5. CARBON STEEL

Carbon is the main alloying element used for hardening and strengthening iron. Spring steels, which are "high-carbon" steels, contain up to about 1.00 percent carbon, and high-carbon tool steels contain from 1.00 to 1.20 percent carbon.

Reading Excerpt

Do not take this as being something of superstition, or as something that would be a good luck charm—but if the entity will wear about its person, or in its pocket, a metal that is carbon steel—preferably in the groin pocket—it will prevent, it will ionize the body—from its very vibrations—to resist cold, congestion, and those inclinations for disturbance with the mucous membranes of the throat and nasal passages.

1842-1, M. 32
born 7/31/07

6. CRYSOLITE

"Chrysolite (olivine) has two distinct methods of occurrence: (a) in igneous rocks, as peridotite, norite, basalt, diabase and gabbro . . . (b) as the product of metamorphism of certain sedimentary rocks containing magnesia and silica . . . " (Dana and Ford, p. 599) Chrysolite is commonly olive green but may range through browns and reds. It exhibits the luster and fracture of glass, and has a hardness of 6 to 7. The clear, green varieties are termed *peridot,* but "peridot" is to be distinguished from "peridot of Brazil" and "peridot of Ceylon," which are tourmalines. Chrysolite occurs in the United States at Thetford, Vermont; Webster, North Carolina; and at a few places in Arizona and New Mexico. Its composition is $(M_9Fe)_2SiO_1$.

"The 'Serpent Isle,' in the Red Sea, was stated by Agatharcides to be the source whence came the topaz (chrysolite); here, by the mandate of the Egyptian kings, the inhabitants collected specimens of this stone for polishing . . . From this Egyptian source, and possibly from others exploited by the Egyptians, have come the finest chrysolites (peridots, or olivines) . . . Chrysolite . . . to exert its full power, is required to be set in gold; worn in this way it dispelled the vague terrors of the night. If, however, it were to be used as a protection from the wiles of evil spirits, the stone had to be pierced and strung on the hair of an ass and then attached to the left arm." (Kunz, pp. 66, 67)

15

See reading 688-1 (p. 4).

7. COPPER

"Pure" *copper* found in nature sometimes contains small amounts of iron, silver, bismuth, tin, lead, or antimony. Its color is copper red; it has a metallic luster and a hardness of 2.5 to 3. Native copper (Cu) usually occurs in beds and veins associated with chalcopyrite, chalcocite, cuprite, malachite, and azurite. In the United States it is found in great abundance on the Keweenaw Peninsula in northern Michigan. Copper crystals are found at Bisbee and Globe, Arizona, and at Georgetown, New Mexico.

Reading Excerpts

As will be, as has been the experience, days and periods, the vibrations from metals and their elements *have* a great deal of influence upon the entity.

Hence as we find, the days close to and upon the thirteenth of October make for the periods when the events, the happenings, the changes, the decisions become as mandatory in the influence of the entity.

It will be found that the odors of henna, with tolu and myrrh, create an influence of ease; while the fire opal, the lapis or copper in its *elemental* form, bring great passion, and intenseness, the abilities to loose emotions through the very centers of the body for the closer association of the spiritual with the activative influences of the mental self.

But the well of truth, yea the fountain of eternal life, wells up from within.

1580-1, F. 48
born 9/21/1890

We find that it would be very helpful for the entity to wear upon the body a piece of stone that is of the lapis lazuli variety, but the essence or fusion of copper; not as a charm but as a helpful force in the vibrations that will coordinate with the body. This worn as a locket or the like would be helpful.

1651-2, F. 49
born 11/6/1889

8. CORAL

Coral consists of "the hard skeletons of certain marine organisms, and its chemical composition is chiefly calcium carbonate ($CaCO_3$). It is secreted from seawater and deposited in the tissues of Anthozoan polyps . . . hydroids . . . and certain algae . . .

"The precious [red; *Corallium rubrum*] coral is found widespread on the borders and around the islands of the Mediterranean Sea. It ranges in depth from shallow water (25 to 50 ft.) to water over 1,000 ft." (Encyclopedia Brittanica, 1956, v. 6, p. 431)

"To still tempests and traverse broad rivers in safety was the privilege of one who bore either red or white coral with him. That this also staunched the flow of blood from a wound, cured madness, and gave wisdom, was said to have been experimentally proved." (Kunz, p. 68)

"Coral, which for twenty centuries or more was classed among the precious stones, to retain its power as an amulet, must not have been worked, and in Italy only such pieces are valued for this purpose as have been freshly gathered from the sea or have been cast up by the sea on the shore." (*ibid.*, p. 69)

"No gem has been more employed as a charm for averting the fell spell of the evil eye than the innocent coral which was credited with the power of destroying the first stroke of the glance, after which it—like the drawn fang of the serpent—was rendered incapable of injury." (Kozminsky, p. 173)

"Plato says: 'Coral is good to be hanged about children's necks, as well as to rub their gums as to preserve them from the falling sickness. It hath also some special sympathy with Nature, for the best coral, being worn about the neck, will turn pale and wan if the party that wears it be sick, and comes to its former colour again as they recover health.'" (*ibid.*, p. 174)

Brown corals are supposed to delight evil spirits, and oriental mystics warn against wearing dull, dirty, or discolored specimens.

Reading Excerpts

Q-7. Are there any colors or jewelry that I should wear in order to have better vibrations? If so, what?

A-7. Any of jewelry or ornaments that are of coral would be well; for this is—as it represents, as it is in itself of Creative Forces, or from the water itself. Red, white or coral in any form.   307-15, F. 60
                                                        born 6/6/1878

Hence we find, because the activities of the entity through the earth have involved and do involve the lives and activities of the many, the elements which are of nature's vibrations would have, do have, much to do with the entity's activity.

Coral should be about the entity at all times; worn—not as a charm, not other than the vibrations of the body as related to same. Because of the very nature of its construction, and the very activity of the soul forces of the entity, this [coral] would become a helpful influence in the experience of the entity. Hence this we would wear about the body, but against the flesh.

All things that have to do with such as marine activities will be a part of the entity's *ultimate* activity in this material experience . . .

For, a birth into materiality is not by chance, but that the will of the Creative Forces may make manifest in the experience of each soul its purpose in a material and mental plane.

Through the very indications of that element as would be helpful in its experience (the coral), we find that the entity is highly sensitive to intuitive forces, spiritual aspects, spiritual imports. 2073-2, F. 40
born 4/28/1900

9. CRYSTAL

Rock crystal is colorless or nearly colorless *quartz*, whether in distinct crystals or not. Its hardness is 7 and, chemically, it is SiO_2. Rock crystal can be found in many localities throughout the world. In the United States, brilliant crystals can be found at Middleville, Ellenville, and Little Falls, New York; "beautiful colorless crystals occur at Hot Springs, Garland Co., Arkansas." (Dana and Ford, p. 474)

The art of crystal-gazing, with an eye toward prophecies, is well known. Kunz (pp. 207-233) has summarized the lore of crystal balls and points out that for "the Japanese, rock-crystal is the 'perfect jewel,' *tama*, it is at once a symbol of purity and of the infinity of space, and also of patience and perseverance . . . " (Kunz, p. 217)

Reading Excerpt

As to the elemental influences having to do with the entity's experience—we find that the crystal as a stone, or any white stone, has a helpful influence—if carried about the body; not as an omen, not merely as a "good luck piece" or "good luck charm" but these vibrations that are needed as helpful influences for the entity are well to be kept close about the body. 2285-1, M. 16
born 5/17/24

10. DIAMOND

Ordinary *diamond* occurs in "crystals usually with rounded faces and varying from those which are colorless and free from flaws (*first water*) through many shades of color, yellow being the most common . . . " (Dana and Ford, p. 395) It has a hardness of 10, being the hardest substance known. A diamond is composed of pure carbon (C), and the name has been derived by corruption from the ancient Greek name for the mineral that meant *the invincible.* Diamonds are found in several countries. They occur mainly in stream deposits (gravels, sands, and silts). In the United States, a few stones have been found in gravels in North Carolina, Georgia, Virginia, Colorado, California, and Wisconsin. Near Murfeesboro, Arkansas, diamonds occur in the soil and a peridotite rock. Africa, Brazil, and India are regions wherein great quantities have been mined.

Kunz relates the following in regard to legends concerning the therapeutic use of the diamond: "In the Babylonian Talmud we read of a marvelous precious stone belonging to Abraham. This was perhaps a diamond, or possibly a pearl . . . the following version represents it to be a diamond: R. Simeon, ben Johanan said, 'A diamond was hanging on Abraham's neck, and when a sick man looked upon it he was cured. And when Abraham passed away, the Lord sealed it in the planet of the sun.'" (Kunz, p. 377)

"The Hindus believed that it was extremely dangerous to use diamonds of inferior quality for curative purposes, as they would not only fail to remedy the disease for which they were prescribed, but might cause lameness, jaundice, pleurisy, and even leprosy." (*ibid.,* p. 378)

"To dream of diamonds was considered symbolical of success, wealth, happiness and victory, and its reputed power of binding man and woman together in happy wedlock has made it a favorite stone for engagement rings, and in some countries for wedding rings." (Kozminsky, p. 203)

Reading Excerpts

In Neptune we find those things of the mystic nature, or the mysterious. Hence we find those things that pertain to amulets, charms, or those things that deal with the influence that arises from the environs of certain kinds of music, all become a portion of the entity's experience . . .

Q-5. Is there any particular stone or stones I should wear?
A-5. Gold in the forms of circles or of many bangles, and the like, are greater [help] to the entity than stones; save diamonds.   852-12, F. 18
                                                           born 6/5/17

Pearls and diamonds are the stones that bring the vibratory reactions and the experiences in the environs of the entity . . .

In the present experience, things pertaining to the oriental *mind* become of special interest to the entity; as also especially the intricate work as carvings, filigree, and activities of such a nature that were a part of the entity's experience through that sojourn. Things overlaid with gold or ivory or coral, things of that nature become a part of the entity's experience—these are innate or manifested by a great influence.

Hence the abilities of the entity in the present to attain or maintain close relationship to vibratory influences and forces, whether they emanate from the mineral, the animal, or the vegetable kingdoms. All of these become innately as portions of the entity's experience.   1847-1, F. 61
born 5/15/1878

Before that the entity was in the Egyptian land when there were those activities in the replenishing or reestablishing of the activities of the Priest with the return from banishment.

The entity was among those set in charge of the preparations of the precious metals; as a carver of gold, a carver of stones— as of rubies, diamonds, emeralds and those [stones] prepared for those in authority and in power.

As each stone indeed has the spirit—as the spirit of the pearl, the spirit of the diamond—it is the fire that may be in a little different vibration, burned—so in its oppression [misuse] it may bring that which fires the imagination of those who are very selfish or it may bring peace to the wearer. The diamond is selfish in its very nature, while you will find that the pearl is a natural consequence of irritation—and it will bring either peace or irritation to the wearer as will the diamond, while all of the others have their varying vibrations as the bloodstone or the others, as the entity has indicated in the things set down during those periods of activity in Egypt as Ark-uen.
3657-1, M. 58
born 11/8/1885

In Venus we find appreciation of beauty, as well as of things. Ye should find the diamond and the ruby close to your body oft, for their vibrations will keep the vibrations of the body in better attune with infinity and not with purely mental or material things of life.   5322-1, F. 47
born 6/18/1897

In Mercury also we find the inclinations for definite divisions of application of the mental self to material things— minerals and their attributes; that is, the *emotions* that arise in the experience from individuals in the variations, as might be said, of carbon; in its variations between coal and a diamond—they are the same, but one is under pressure, the other is with water!   1561-1, M. 57
born 9/6/1880

11. EMERALD

Emerald is the clear, emerald green variety of *beryl,* and should not be confused with the *oriental emerald* of jewelry, which is an emerald-colored sapphire. The emerald's coloration is due to small amounts of chromium. Its physical and chemical properties are those of beryl (see p. 12). Good emeralds are not common in the United States; the most famous locality for emeralds in the world is Muso, Colombia.

Therapeutic uses of the emerald were largely as an antidote for poisons and as a deterrent for possession by demons. They were also used in the treatment of diseases of the eye. Emeralds found in the workings of the old Kleopatra mines are of the lighter or beryl variety. "These gems were much sought after in ancient times, the Egyptian women being esteemed the best searchers 'because of their superior eyesight.'" (Kozminsky, p. 141)

Reading Excerpts

See readings 3657-1 (p. 20) and 5294-1 (p. 14).

12. GOLD

Native *gold* (Au) is usually alloyed with silver in varying amounts and sometimes contains traces of copper or iron. It has a hardness of 2.5 to 3, metallic luster, and gold yellow color. Gold is widely distributed throughout the world, being most frequently found in quartz veins and various placer deposits. The main occurrences of gold in the United States are summarized by Dana and Ford (p. 403). An unusually large deposit is known to be present at Fort Knox, Kentucky.

Reading Excerpts

See readings 852-12 (p. 19) and 1931-1 (p. 24).

13. LAPIS LAZULI
(Lazurite)

Lapis Lazuli, or *lazurite,* is a massive, compact stone that ranges in color from rich Berlin blue or azure blue, through violet blue and greenish blue. Its hardness is 5 to 5.5 and its composition is essentially $3NaAlSiO_4.Na_2S$. Lazurite is probably always a contact metamorphic mineral and usually occurs in limestones near granitic rock masses. It commonly encloses small grains of pyrite. Lapis lazuli (lazurite) is found in Afghanistan, Turkestan, Persia, Italy, and Chile. It occurs in the United States on Italian Mountain, Gunnison County, Colorado.

In ancient Egypt and Babylonia, lapis lazuli was highly valued. In Egypt, for instance, pieces of lapis lazuli were inscribed with certain chapters of the Book of the Dead, a very ancient book whose chapters describe the passage of the soul of the deceased through the realm of the dead. "The form of an eye, fashioned out of lapis-lazuli and ornamented with gold, constituted an amulet of great power; it was inscribed with the 140th chapter of the Book of the Dead. On the last day of the month Mechir, an offering 'of all things good and holy' was to be made before this symbolic eye, for on that day the supreme god Ra was believed to place such an image upon his head." (Kunz, p. 229) "A notable instance of the use of lapis-lazuli in ancient Egypt was as the material for the image of Truth (*Ma*), which the Egyptian chief-justice wore on his neck, suspended from a golden chain." (*ibid.*, p. 119)

Some authorities consider the lapis lazuli the 5th, and others the 11th, stone of the magic breastplate. An old tradition states that the tables of the Law of Moses were inscribed on two blocks of lapis lazuli. This stone was also used in ceremonies in the Temple of Heaven in China, "and the Chinese sacred writings record how at one time the priest-kings bore it as an offering to the Lord of the Universe." (Kozminsky, p. 255)

Ancient physicians used the gem to treat eye trouble, and the old alchemists appear to have alluded to it as the Stone of Heaven.

Reading Excerpts

In giving that which may be helpful for this entity in this experience, [we give] not only from the astrological sojourn of the entity in the environs about the earth—that have been accredited by the ancients to those influences upon the earth, the activative forces in their positions about the earth—but those things that are more as omens, the various accredited vibrations as in stones, etc., [which] we find having an influence upon the entity. For the entity should ever wear about the body the lapis lazuli or the lapis linguis; for these will bring strength to the body through those vibrations that are brought or built in the innate experience of the entity from its sojourn in the Egyptian land . . .

But wear the stone ever about the body, and *touching* the body.

691-1, F. 34
born 4/11/1900

Q-7. If I were to wear the stone [lapis lazuli or lapis linguis], as suggested in a previous reading, would it improve my mental, physical or spiritual condition?

A-7. This naturally is to make, as indicated, the body more sensitive to the higher vibrations. Not so much in the physical health as in the mental and spiritual influences, that would be materially aided.

691-2, F. 34
born 4/11/1900

As to stones—have near to self, wear preferably upon the body, about the neck, the lapis lazuli; this preferably encased in crystal. It will be not merely as an ornament but as strength from the emanation which will be gained by the body always from same. For the stone is itself an emanation of vibrations of the elements that give vitality, virility, strength, and that of assurance in self.

1981-1, F. 19
born 12/9/20

Symbols and such activities have always meant something to the entity. Hence certain characters of adornments would be well about the entity. Keep something blue, and especially the color and emanations of the lapis lazuli [about the body]; not the slick or polished nature, but of that nature that the emanations from same may give life and vitality.

2132-1, F. 70
born 9/9/1870

Q-4. *Any color, stone or symbol for spiritual development?*
A-4. The lapis lazuli should be the better, but this should be encased and worn—for this body—about the waist; not around your neck.

3053-3, F. 11
born 2/19/32

Q-8. *Please give my . . . stone . . .*
A-8. The lapis lazuli, worn close to the body would be well for the general health of the body—and this you will have to be careful of very soon. The lapis lazuli, of course, is an erosion of copper; but this encased in a glass and worn about the body would be well.

3416-1, F. 40
born 1/15/04

Q-7. *Is the stone which I found in Alaska last summer the lapis linguis?*
A-7. Lapis langis, lapis lazuli. This as we find might be said to be a part of that same composition referred to; for it carries that vibration which will give strength to the body. Well that this be preserved between thin layers of glass or such compositions, else its radiation is too great.

1931-2, M. 20
born 9/11/19

See readings 707-1 (p. 11), 3416-1 (p. 5), 2282-1 (p. 14), and 1580-1 (p. 16).

14. LAPIS LIGURIUS
(Malachite?)

Malachite, a bright green mineral, is very probably the "lapis ligurius" mentioned in the following reading (an alternative could be *chrysocolla).* Malachite occurs in crystals of adamantine luster, or in dull, earthy masses. The hardness of malachite is 3.5 to 4 and its chemical composition is $CuCO_3.Cu(OH)_2$. This common ore of copper is found in the United States in Berks County, Pennsylvania; Ducktown, Tennessee; Bisbee, Arizona; Good Springs, Nevada; Mineral Point, Wisconsin; Butte, Montana; and the Lake Superior copper district, to mention only a few localities. It often occurs together with azurite, "lapis linguis," and their origin is the same; that is, by progression through limestones of copper solutions.

Malachite was procured by the ancient Egyptians from mines between Suez and Sinai as early as 4000 B.C. They held it to be useful in the treatment of cholera and rheumatism. In the Middle Ages it was especially treasured as a protection against the "evil eye." The modern name "malachite" is derived from the Greek *malache,* "marsh mallow, from its resemblance to the soft green leaves of this plant." (Kozminsky, p. 261)

Reading Excerpts

As to the material inclinations—we find things that become what might be termed as omens. Not that these should be merely considered as good luck stones that the entity should wear about self often, or most always—but the lapis ligurius would bring much that will act in that manner as would be termed a *protective* influence, if kept about the entity. This is the green stone, you see—the crystallization of copper and those influences that are creative within themselves . . .

For, as indicated from the influence of the lapis ligurius, there is the need for not only the copper ore, that is a part of man's *own* development in many fields, but the need for the very combination of its elements as *protection* to not only the material benefits but the bodily forces necessary for the transmission of benefits through its own physical being.

For, the very elements of body—through which spirit and mind manifest—are atomic in their nature. Hence so are the elements of this stone indicated, that partakes of most of the elements that are to man of great influence or power, because of their representation in the body.

Hence the radial activity of radium, as well as the strengthening influences of gold, the stabilizing influence of silver, are all a part of those elements that make for the transmission through the activity of the very vibratory forces themselves, and become to *this* body of great influence; for this entity is not only destined but rather prone to be thrown *into* those channels where all of such are necessary for usage in either the protection or destruction of mankind himself. As to which—the entity will choose, for it is within his own power.

1931-1, M. 20
born 9/11/19

Q-5. Where may I find the stone lapis lazuli or lapis ligurius?
A-5. This is an exuding of copper. Either in the copper mines of the southwest, or about Superior, or in Montana.

1931-3, M. 20
born 9/11/19

15. LAPIS LINGUIS
(Azurite)

Azurite ("lapis linguis"), like malachite ("lapis ligurius"), is a mineral of secondary origin, being found in the upper oxidized portions of ore deposits. "It has been formed either by the action of carbonated waters upon copper compounds or by copper solutions upon limestones." (Dana and Ford, p. 528) It is almost always associated with malachite. Azurite is invariably some shade of *blue,* and occurs in either crystals or dull masses. It has a hardness of 3.5 to 4 and its formula is $2CuCO_3.Cu(OH)_2$. It occurs in significant amounts only at Bisbee and Morenci, Arizona, and at Kelly, New Mexico.

Azurite was known to Pliny as *caeruleum.* Very little mention is made of this gem by the many modern authors who have reported on the ancient and medieval uses of gems and stones. It is possible, therefore, that its use was restricted largely to prehistoric times, or that its properties were a closely guarded secret.

Reading Excerpts

Q-9. Do you advise a trip to Arizona this winter?
A-9. Be very good, and especially if you'll seek some of these stones that may be found in some of these portions; for this country is full of those things in which the body is interested in these directions. Lapis lingua [?].
Q-10. During which months?
A-10. February and March.
Q-11. To what stones do you refer?
A-11. The lapis lingua [?]. It's blue!
Q-12. Of what value is it?
A-12. Of particular value to those who are interested in things psychic!
Read what was in the first effort that was made, as to all

those that used the stones as settings to induce influences from without that would aid an individual in its contact with the higher sources of activity!   440-2, M. 23
                                                                                                born 4/24/10

Q-7. Having recommended a stay in Arizona this winter, suggest the most suitable place for the periods mentioned.
A-7. Either Phoenix or Prescott, particularly if there is to be the seeking for the indicated conditions in the country. [At] Phoenix, and north and west from there, at not great distances, may be found two or three various deposits of the lapis that may be found to be most beneficial in many of the exerimentations in which the body is particularly interested. Ringle, in this particular portion of the country, is interested in mines of various characters, but don't be carried off by him into gold prospecting, or into the searching for the more precious gems. For, lapis is not considered a high quality of gem; rather a very low form, but for that indicated in the character of the stone itself, it would be most helpful in creating that vibration which will make for developments of certain characters of demonstrations with any psychic forces or psychic individuals.

This may be—will be—a very interesting experiment for the body. Go to the New York Museum of Natural History. Sit by a large quantity of this type of stone and listen at it sing! Do it in the open! Don't let others make a fool of you, or their remarks overcome you—but sit by it and listen at it sing; for it does! It's from Arizona.

Q-8. Would you suggest any particular ranch in Arizona?
A-8. We have suggested here a contact which will not only be all over ranches, but rather a contact that would be very good for seeking out in *any* field of activity!

Q-9. Describe these stones so that the body may be able to locate them.
A-9. Go and look at them in the museum!

Q-10. How should they be set and cut?
A-10. As pendant, either on wrist and worn on body or around the waist.

Q-11. What results may we expect from such setting and cutting?
A-11. Now we are going backwards from what we have given! These, as indicated, are not the channels to be relied upon except in creating the atmosphere. The same thing may be done with an oak tree, or with a persimmon tree—but the activities that come about are because of the emanations thrown off from the stones themselves to the active forces in the body itself!

Q-12. We are told these stones are located in the Colorado river beds. Is this correct?
A-12. They may be found in Colorado river beds, yes—but there's acres of them in other places than river beds!

Now, in connection with these, there may be found [other examples] of more precious stones—but *do not* be carried off in seeking these, because you are going into a country and into a field where *later* the interest may be turned, but not in the particular period through February and March!

440-3, M. 23
born 4/24/10

Mrs. Cayce: You will have before you the body and inquiring mind of [440] . . . also the information given this entity through this channel in a recent series of readings, together with his endeavors to follow out some of the suggestions given him, to seek the lapis lingua in the Museum of Natural History in New York. You will answer the questions which he has submitted.

Mr. Cayce: . . . In the seeking, as was given in the information, the lapis—not lapis lingua, because that is different but of the same formation, or comes from the same formation—but the lapis is there, in the hall—north side—front of the north window, in the mineral divisions here—large blue stone. It weighs nearly a ton and has many facets, in the manner in which it was removed from the mines; is from Arizona, and the color necessary for use as instructed—may be seen by stopping below or getting the light through a portion of the upper part, though—to be sure—it's very much thicker than would be necessary for use. It's there! Not lapis linguis, but *lapis!*

Ready for questions.

Q-1. Under what name is it catalogued? Please spell the entire name.

A-1. L-a-p-i-s.

Q-2. From what place in Arizona is it listed as having come?

A-2. Nearer Tucson.

Q-3. Is this stone to be found in the Morgan wing of the Natural History Museum of N.Y.?

A-3. In the mineral—the general mineral division. See, there isn't such a far distance removed—only about six feet—from a stellyte [selenite? stalactite?] which also comes from Arizona, one of the largest in the museum. It is cinder, of course.

Q-4. Spell the word lingua.

A-4. It's been given. Look it up! Do something for yourself!

440-9, M. 23
born 4/24/10

Q-4. In relation to the lapis, I found a 9000-lbs. stone enclosed in a glass case, etc. Is this the one referred to?

A-4. This, as we find, is the one referred to—though it has been moved from its former location or surroundings, but is in general in the same—*and* the stone as referred to.

. . . the lapis linguis is that name which was implied to touchstones, or those used by initiates in their various ceremonial activities . . . [and] those that are of a psychic turn may hear the emanations as retained or thrown off by influences about such stones. They are of semi-gem or semi-value to . . . those that have not as yet comprehended . . . the value of such stones in relationships to such conditions for those that are not gifted or those that are not so sensitive as to be able to hear those vibrations given off, or the singing or talking of stones—as they have been called in places. Yet, as has been indicated for this body, there should be—there is—the ability within this body . . . to hear the singing or the movements [of the lapis] . . . Lapis linguis is that one that has been in use or in touch with those whose vibrations or emanations or auras are of such natures as to have given those vibrations in the nature that any portion of such a stone may give off that which may be heard, see?

Q-5. Will it being in a glass case interfere with my hearing it sing?

A-5. It should not interfere wholly, though it will not be heard—to be sure—through the glass as definitely as were it separated.

Q-6. This stone contains malachite and azurite. Is the lapis linguis either of these?

A-6. The azurite.

Q-7. Where will I find this stone in Arizona?

A-7. As indicated, about the place as given—in a ranch—a hundred to a hundred and twenty-five miles north to northwest of the place. Many various characters of this lapis may be found in Arizona, as may be of other stones in the same vicinity of a semiprecious value or nature, but those that are of the greater value as the touchstones or those that may receive (we are putting it in another form or manner) a blessing and transmit same to another, or a curse and transmit same to another, will be found in the nature where the greater portion of the azurite is evidenced in the immediate vicinity.

Q-8. How will I know when I have found this stone that is most useful for my purposes?

A-8. When there is found that [specimen] which is sufficiently clear for the transmission of light and that which may be held in the hand for five to ten minutes and then set aside and listening hear the movements or the vibrations given off from the emanations from self.

Q-9. Should it be translucent . . . ?

A-9. Should be transparent, or sufficient for the light to pass through.

Q-10. Should this touch the skin in wearing it?

A-10. To be sure. Usually worn, of course, around the neck or over the body close to the vibrations from the heart or from the breast itself in its vibrations.

Q-11. Would it not be best over the lyden gland?

A-11. Not be best over the lyden gland, for too great emanations from its surroundings might influence the body itself. You are used to influence the stone to an effect, either upon those to whom it [the stone] may be given or to bring for self the ability to aid in its abilities as raising the vibrations for self. Hence would come over this particular portion, or if desired—for the better in training of self—held over that portion of the hollow on the left side above . . . the collarbone.

Q-12. What is the best method of cutting, and what metals should be used in mounting?

A-12. Use in cutting the ordinary use for the precious or semiprecious stones, in whatever shapes or forms—that are usually the larger in the center and tapering towards the outer edge. Of course, not too large for the use to be worn. The mountings would be white gold or silver.   440-11, M. 23
born 4/24/10

Q-17. It is not the intention of the following questions to criticize, but rather to obtain a greater understanding of the source of this information. First, how do you explain the discrepancies in a description of the lapis in the N.Y. Museum of Natural History as to its weight, color and name by which it is catalogued?

A-17. Discrepancies? The lapis itself, as is seen, is *as* has been given; that there are other minerals or other character of minerals associated with same—Use some imagination! or, as we would give from here, some common reasoning! For, lapis was what was sought for! That's what we were telling you about! That you became associated with same is to be known and used; not used as criticism nor as fault-finding. Oft we may find, in seeking through channels of such natures as these, that there are seeming discrepancies—but if there is sought in sincerity that which is aidful, use the aidful to help self and also aid the sources that you are using as a means of gratifying self's own desires. For, when desires of a seeker are in accord with constructive influences, and the information is sought from the channels or sources that may be in the same manner of seeking to aid and help, if such information is used as contradictory—or to produce or bring in self's own mind controversy, the rebound is upon your source of supply. Do not ever hinder or abuse same! This is not as a fault; rather attempting in the same manner that is being asked as to how to be, or to use that which may be given as being sacred! If not, don't seek it, for your own good—for the good of that which may give same! Who, what or where is such being given you in the present? Read the preface to Dana's *Geology!** [1863, p. ix]
440-12, M. 23
born 4/24/10

*The following paragraph is found in the preface to *only* the first edition of Dana's *Manual of Geology:* "Geology is rapidly taking its place as an introduction to the higher history of man. If the author has sought to exalt a favorite science, it has been with the desire that man—in whom geological history had its consummation, the prophecies of the successive ages their fulfillment—might better comprehend his own nobility and the true purpose of his existence."

Those influences that are emblematical or are of the earth's environs, that will make for omens or helpful influences, are apparent from the entity's activities in sojourns in the earth.

Hence, as we would find, the wearing of the stone lapis linguis would be as an aid in its meditative periods, and would become as a helpful influence. Not as that of "lucky," but rather that as of a helpful influence towards making for the ability to make decisions in dealing with mental attributes.

1058-1, F. 22
born 11/12/13

See reading 691-1 (p. 22).

16. MOONSTONE

Moonstone is a variety of adularia, which in turn is a variety of *orthoclase*. It exhibits a pearly opalescent reflection or a delicate play of colors. "The moonstone, with its moonlike, silvery-white light, changes on the surface as the light varies. This is due to a chatoyancy produced by a reflection caused by certain cleavage planes present in feldspar of the variety [orthoclase] to which the moonstone belongs." (Kunz, p. 334) The color may be gray, white, and pale yellow, or it may be colorless. Its hardness is 6 and it is pure or nearly pure $KAlSi_3O_8$. "The original adularia (Adular) is from the St. Gotthard region in Switzerland. Valencianite, from the silver mine of Valencia, Mexico, is adularia." (Dana and Ford, p. 538).

Moonstone is so abundant in Ceylon that it is called the "Ceylon Opal." "It is related that Pope Leo X possessed a wonderful specimen which, obscure and dull when the moon was old, increased in brilliance as that orb grew from new to full. It is recommended that in order to know the future and to obtain spiritual guidance a moonstone be held in the mouth, under a waning moon. It is also necessary to be quite alone and to send out a mental prayer to the angel Gabriel (angel of the Moon) asking help by God's grace. The Moonstone was considered as a charm against cancer, dropsy, and affections of a watery nature." (Kozminsky, p. 266)

Reading Excerpts

In giving that as may be helpful to this entity in the present, know that the records that are made by an entity in its activities in the earth are the reflection of that the entity has done about its knowledge, its understanding of Creative Forces in the relations of self to the fellow man.

About the entity we find much that may be indicative of those influences in the earth that are as the appearances. These, as we find, bespeak of associations with heraldry, banners, swords, stays and the like; the shield with the bow, the coloring and the reflection of green fields and woods. And the clash that is made in resistances of individuals as to purposefulness, force, power, might of main, becomes associated with the entity.

From those experiences we find that omens arise. Not that they influence, but create by their *vibration* an element through which the *mental* and the spiritual forces of the entity may vibrate for constructive experience in their activity.

The pearl and the moonstone, these in combination or in their setting alone, are well to have about the body.

1037-1, F. 49
born 7/1/1886

Hence the opal that is called the change, with the moonstone, should be stones about the body of entity oft. Wear the fire opal as a locket about the neck. This would be well. Not upon the hands nor upon the wrists, but about the neck.

Wear the others, as of the pearl with moonstone or the like, as rings or amulets or anklets; but never those upon the neck or in the ears—rather upon the extremities; for they will make for bringing out—in the experiences of those the entity meets— those very colors and vibrations that have been indicated to which the entity is so sensitive . . .

Q-8. To what color do I vibrate?

A-8. As has been indicated, all colors almost fade when the entity enters. It gives life then to any; but those that are of the bright colors, yet those that are in harmony, are those that should be most about the body.

1406-1, F. 14
born 2/2/23

In the material things—wear as an ornament, preferably a ring, the moonstone; and have the activities of all the influences of metals, especially the platinum, about thee. Their vibrations are in accord with that to keep thy animation in accord with the best thou mayest accomplish.

1620-2, F. 45
born 9/22/1893

For the entity was among those who had come from portions of Alabama and settled in what is now Arkansas (or Ar-Kansas as then called); and the entity was among those who panned for gold and found diamonds.

But the entity learned from those experiences that which would be well for the body. While it should never wear a great deal of jewelry—it doesn't fit the universality of mind of the entity, nor does the vibration of jewelry (cheap or good) mean much to the entity, but—wear the moonstone close to your body, or on your body. It will give strength, and it will keep that which is nearest to you closer to you; not as an omen but as a part of your mental and spiritual consciousness. Have same

as a chain, or upon a chain, about your neck; not as an ornament, but rather as a helpmeet, as an urge, as a vibration that will be most helpful—as it was in the experience in that land as Margaret Fitzhugh.   5125-1, F. 30
born 10/28/13

See reading 5294-1 (p. 14).

17. OPAL

Opal is composed of silica, like quartz, but with a varying amount of water $(SiO_2.nH_2O)$. *Precious opal* exhibits a play of delicate colors, and the *fire opal* displays "hyacinth red to honey yellow colors, with firelike reflections, somewhat irised on turning." (Dana and Ford, p. 476) Hardness of the opal is 5.5 to 6.5 and it usually occurs in a massive form. *Common opal* is widespread in its occurrence. Gem opal is found in Humbolt County, Nevada, and fire opal at Hidalgo, Mexico.

In Pliny's words, "The opal is made up of the glories of the most precious gems which make description so difficult. For amongst them is the gentler fire of the ruby, the rich purple of the amethyst, the sea green of the emerald, glittering together in union indescribable. Others by the intensity of their hues equal all the painters' colours ... " In the ancient world the opal was thought to favor "children, the theatre, amusements, friendships, and feelings. Held between the eyes it gave proper direction to thoughts. Held in the left hand and gazed upon it favored the desires. It is the stone of hope and achievement and has been truly described as the 'gem of the gods.' Above all, it is a stone of love, but if the lover be false its influence is reversed, and the opal proves a sorry gem for faithless lovers." (Kozminsky, p. 291)

Reading Excerpts

Q-4. Will wearing opals by one who does not have them as birth stone signify ill omens for that person?

A-4. No. No, opals will be helpful if there is kept the correct attitude, for it will enable the entity to hold on to self or to prevent those who would be angry from flying off the handle too much.   4006-1, F. 41
born 6/18/02

Before that we find the entity was in the land now known as or called the Egyptian, when those peoples began the interpretations and the applications of the truths that were gathered from the Atlanteans.

The *entity* came into the experience in Egypt but was of the Atlantean peoples, and interpreted in the Temple Beautiful

those beauties of the temples in Poseidia; for from there we find those great lights—opaline lights, as it were—about the entity. And these, as we find, would be those stones that to others may bring as mystery yet the fire opal would be of the stones that should be about the entity; for the holding of that fire, that vigor, that *understanding* that makes for purification, even though the fires of the flesh must be *burned out* that the glory of self may be made manifest in being a channel for the glory of the living truths to be known and experienced among others.　　　　　　　　　**1193-1, F. 15**
born 8/23/20

See readings 5294-1 (p. 14), 1406-1 (p. 31), and 1580-1 (p. 16).

18. PEARL

"A natural pearl is a concretion formed by a mollusc; it consists of the same material as the mollusc's shell. Every mollusc endowed with a shell—not only the marine pearl oysters and the fresh-water pearly mussels—can produce pearls . . . pearls are understood to be globular concretions . . . provided with qualities such as iridescence and translucence, which make them desirable and often highly prized gems; the more perfect the shape (symmetrical ball or droplike) and the deeper the pearly lustre, the more the pearl is esteemed . . . The chemical composition of gem pearls is carbonate of chalk (about 92%), organic substance (about 6%) and water (2%). The hardness varies from 2.5 to 4.5 . . . " (*Encyclopedia Britannica,* 1956, v. 17, pp. 420-421)

"Give not that which is holy unto the dogs, neither cast ye your pearls before swine . . . "(Matthew 7:6)

"Again, the kingdom of heaven is like unto a merchant man, seeking goodly pearls . . . "
(Matthew 13:45)

The ancient Hindus included the pearl among the five precious stones in the magical necklace of Vishnu, the other four being the diamond, ruby, emerald, and sapphire. "The golden pearl was the emblem of wealth, the white of idealism, the black of philosophy, the pink of beauty, the red of health and energy, the grey of thought. Lusterless pearls are considered unfortunate, as also are pearls that have lost their sheen when on a dying person's finger, as sometimes happens." (Kozminsky, p. 327) Swedenborg wrote that pearls were Truth and the knowledge of truth, celestial and spiritual knowledge, faith and charity. "The pearl was esteemed as the emblem of purity, innocence and peace, and was sacred to the Moon and Diana. For this reason in ancient times it was worn by young girls and virgins on whom the protection of 'chaste Diana' was invoked ... As a cure for irritability it was ground to a fine powder and a quantity, seldom more than a grain, was drunk in new milk." (*ibid.*, p. 327)

Reading Excerpts

The pearl should be worn upon the body, or against the flesh of the body; for its vibrations are healing, as well as creative—because of the very irritation as produced same, as a defense in the mollusk that produced same.

Those activities of the body pertaining to the emotions are well within the experience—whether for physical exercise or for strengthening of the poise.   951-4, F. 25
born 4/29/14

Q-2. My life reading suggested the wearing of pearls next to my skin for the healing vibration. Does the pearl necklace I'm now wearing help or hinder?

A-2. When its vibrations have taken the body-forces, it will be well. Or if the body would demagnetize the necklace as it is, it would be more helpful for the body. Do not touch with same, but expose necklace to the ultraviolet ray for one-tenth of a second, or as a flash. This will demagnetize it and set it for better body vibration for this body.   951-6, F. 25
born 4/29/14

The entity gained throughout that experience. And, as indicated, that which would be called the flag or the emblem of the king—as given to Nehemiah then—should be a portion of those influences about the entity in the present; that which is now more closely depicted in the Maltese cross that is only half of same, with the crown overlapping same in purple and in blue. These should be the colors about the entity, as should be the stones of the ruby and the pearl. For these have their influences; the purity of the pearl, though under stress it may come into being; the valor and the strength that is imparted in the inner influence of the ruby about the body.
1144-2, F. 46
born 4/22/1890

From the sojourns of the entity in Neptune we find rather the influences of water, as well as things coming from water, are a part of the entity's experience.

Thus the entity should ever keep a pearl about the self or upon the person, not only for the material vibration but for the ideal expression. For, it will be an omen—not only because of the vibrations that it may give to self but because of keeping the even temperament, yea the temper itself. For the entity can get mad, and when it is mad it is really *mad!*

This arises more from the material sojourns than the astrological—for these [pitfalls] the entity chose to meet in the material rather than the fourth and fifth dimensional phase of its activities. . .

Before that the entity was in the Persian land, during those periods when there arose the turmoils between the bedouins or Arabians and those of the Persian land; when the activities of Croesus made for the greater rule through the eastern portion, extending to the great sea.

The entity was an interpreter, and might be called the keeper of the treasury for Croesus. For, the entity analyzed the ability of the peoples of the various lands—as to how, in what manner, in what form, tax or payments for the upkeep of the land might be best brought from the varied groups.

Thus the entity became an interpreter of signs, as well as of the mysteries and stories of the East; and the entity in that experience *owned* the larger collection of pearls from the Persian Gulf and area—which is still the source of the most beautiful of these precious stones.

Keep such an one about the body, not only because of the vibrations but because of the abilities indicated. For, as is realized—and is oft analyzed by the entity—this [the pearl] is among those precious stones that indicates in its formation, in its beauty, the hardships overcome by the very source that made the beauty of the stone itself . . .

Q-5. What hobbies will benefit me most in developing any latent talent or ability I may possess?

A-5. The study of stones—especially precious stones. Not necessarily the owning of same, but what part they have played, do play—not in the lives of the idle rich, nor of those so begone by carnal forces; rather that ye may gain by keeping a pearl close about thy body.　　　　　　　　2533-1, M. 36
born 12/22/04

Q-6. What colors, stones, odors, and musical notes are best for me?

A-6. The music as of the pastoral nature; that is, as attuning to the vibration of flowers, the song of birds, the wind, the hail, the sleet, the snow. These in their roughness, yea in their quietness. All of these are appealing.

The colors—mauve and violet. These are the better for the body—they are healing to the body.

The stone—the pearl should be worn close to the body; not as an ornament, but rather as that which gives strength to the body.　　　　　　　　3374-1, F. 35
born 8/21/08

See readings 275-31 (p. 13), 1037-1 (p. 31), 1406-1 (p. 31), and 1847-1 (p. 20).

19. PLATINUM

Native *platinum* is whitish steel-gray in color and has a metallic luster. It has a hardness of 4.0 to 4.5, is sometimes magnetic, and usually occurs in grains and scales. This mineral is rare. In the United States, it occurs in the gold sands of Rutherford and Burke Counties, North Carolina, and in the black sands of a number of California placers.

Reading Excerpt

See reading 1620-2 (p. 31).

20. RUBY

The ruby is a variety of *corundum* that is ruby red in color. Other varieties of corundum are sapphire and emery, and all of them have a hardness of 9 (next in hardness to diamond). The composition of the ruby (corundum) is Al_2O_3. Rubies are found in the United States at Amity, New York and at Vernon, New Jersey. They usually occur, in place, as accessory minerals in crystalline rocks.

"The ruby has many names in Sanskrit, some of them clearly showing that it was more valued as a gem by the Hindus than any other. For instance, it is called *ratnaraj,* 'king of precious stones,' and *ratnanayaka,* 'leader of precious stones'; another name, applied to a particular shade of ruby, is *padmaraga,* 'red as the lotus.' " (Kunz, p. 101) "To dream of a ruby indicated to the businessman rich patronage and success in trade, to the farmer a successful harvest and to the professional man elevation or fame and success in different degrees. It was always considered more fortunate to wear the ruby on the left hand or left side of the body." (Kozminsky, p. 350)

Reading Excerpts

Q-5. Is there a stone or ring somewhere waiting for me, that I should wear? What causes the feeling that there is, and what power has such a stone in reference to one's life?

A-5. That has been builded by the knowledge which has come to self oft, as to the influences that are *without* self. That thoughts are things and may be miracles or crimes is true. So, the experiences have brought that; as to how those things in their various emanations of the cosmic or etheric forces in nature gather about them—as in stones—a concentration of a force or power.

The ruby would make for the body that not as something

which would be other than the power that self attributes to same, through its actual experience. But the light or reflection from same [the ruby], worn on hand or body, will enable the body to concentrate in its mental application the greater—through the influences such a stone brings to material expression.

How? Each element, each stone, each variation of stone, has its own atomic movement, held together by the units of energy that in the universe are concentrated in that particular activity. Hence they come under varied activities according to their color, vibration or emanation.

In this particular one (the ruby) there is that fitness with that which has been the experience of *this* soul, this entity, through material expression. Hence it is an aid, a crutch to lean upon. But, as has always been given, let it be a stepping-stone; *not* that which thou *standest* only upon!   531-3, M. 40
born 12/6/1893

Q-7. What is my seal? Please give interpretation.

A-7. The tree—as of the bay tree; with the cross and the cup *on* same. The cross on the trunk, the cup or the chalice in the foliage. The words as would be with same, Ixcel Tum Ken; the interpretation: "Grow in strength, in might, as the tree; but in the *Lord* as thy guide."

This should be in color, to be sure, as the bay tree—and the chalice or cup red, while the cross would be *green*.

The stones that should be about the body would be of the ruby; the color or the cloth as should be most used would be purple and mauve—these should ever be. And wear something *blue* ever next to the body.   1222-1, F. 34
born 1/18/02

See readings 1144-2 (p. 34), 1616-1 (p. 13), 1770-2 (p. 13), 3657-1 (p. 20), and 5322-1 (p. 20).

21. SARDONYX

The sardonyx is cryptocrystalline *quartz*. It is like onyx in that its different colored layers are in even planes and the banding is straight. It differs, however, in that it includes layers of clear red to brownish red chalcedony (carnelian, sard), along with other layers of white, brown, and sometimes black-colored material. Sardonyx has a hardness of 7 and its chemical formula is SiO_2. The coloration is probably due mainly to small amounts of iron.

Swedenborg is reported to have seen in the sardonyx the "Love of Good and Light." "It exhibits sard and white chalcedony in layers, but some ancient authors account as fine only those specimens which exhibit three layers at least, a black base, a white zone and a layer of red or brown—the black symbolizing humility, the white virtue, and the red fearlessness ... In the Rosicrucian jewels the sardonyx appears as the gem of victorious ecstasy and rapture which flow from the eternal font of delight, banishing grief and woe. It was said to give self-control, conjugal happiness and good fortune, and it is said that if the woman, whose talismanic stone it is, neglects to wear it, she will never marry." (Kozminsky, p. 283)

Reading Excerpt

Well that there be carried on the person the sardonyx stone (that is, in its semiprecious state); either in statuettes, pins, buttons, or a piece of same carried. Not as a protection but rather for the vibratory forces that influence the choices made by the mental forces of the entity itself. Statuettes, frames or the like are well. Much of the same vibrations may be obtained from using those combinations of stone made from the soya bean; which may act in much the same capacity. Figures made of same are well to have about the entity's *sleeping* quarters or abode.   **1528-1, M. 24**
                                              born 10/23/14

SCARAB

The scarab is not a stone; rather, it is the *engraving* of the form of a certain beetle, *Scarabaeus sacer,* upon a stone. "This presupposes a considerable development of civilization, since the art of engraving on precious stones offers many mechanical difficulties and thus requires a high degree of artistic and mechanical skill. It is true that the earliest engraved stones, the Babylonian cylinders and the Egyptian scarabs, were both designed to serve an eminently practical purpose as well, namely, that of seals; but in a great number of instances these primitive seals were looked upon as endowed with a talismanic power, and were worn on the person as talismans.

"A curious symbolism induced the Egyptians to find in this beetle an emblem of the world of fatherhood and of man. The round ball wherein the eggs were deposited typified the world, and, as the Egyptians thought that the scarabaei were all males, this especially signified the male principle in generation, becoming types of fatherhood and man. At the same time, as only full-grown beetles were observed, it was believed these creatures represented a regeneration or reincarnation, since it was not realized that the eggs or larval and pupa stages had anything to do with the generation of the beetle ...

"While, however, this was the popular view, it seems unlikely that such close observers as were the more cultured Egyptians should have been entirely unfamiliar with the real genesis of the *Scarabaeus sacer;* but, in this case also, there would have been no difficulty in finding it emblematic of immortality . . . The larval stage might well signify the mortal life; the pupa stage, the intermediate period represented by the mummy . . . and, lastly, the fully developed beetle could be regarded as a type of the rebirth into everlasting life . . .

"Scarabs are frequently engraved with the hieroglyph *anch,* meaning 'life,' and *ha,* meaning 'increase of power' . . . The emblem of stability . . . (*tet*) is also employed . . ."(Kunz, pp.115-116) An exhaustive treatment of scarabs is given in Ward (1902).

Reading Excerpt

In the one before this we find [the entity] in that land known as the Egyptian. The entity [was] then in the household of the priest, and of those that waited on the companion of the priest. In the name Is-Eli. In this experience the entity rose to power, position, place, fame, through the experiences in that period, as related to the various manners of expression of praise in music, in art, and *especially* in that of placing of stones. In the present, the innate desire to feel precious stones, to compare same, to watch the change in the color in same, is seen from *this* experience. These will make for much *judgment* to the entity, and the beryl and scarab should be a portion of the entity's dress, *ever;* either worn as the amulet, the ring, or such, will make for a safety in the entity's present experience.

1719-1, M. 10
born 6/19/20

22. TOPAZ

The mineral, *topaz,* commonly exhibits the following colors: "straw yellow, wine yellow, white, grayish, greenish, bluish, reddish." (Dana and Ford, p. 613) Its hardness is 8 and its luster vitreous. The formula for topaz can be written $[Al(F,OH)_2]AlSiO_4$. Topaz occurs in the rocks of the granite family, in veins and in cavities. In the United States, topaz crystals of gem quality occur in the Pike's Peak region in Colorado, at Streeter, Texas, and in Juab County, Utah.

"The Sanscrit word *topas,* meaning heat, may well describe the topaz, the color of which can be changed readily by heat, and which, under heat, pressure, and friction, exhibits strong electric phenomena.

"The power of the topaz was said to increase as the moon increased, especially if the night orb was at new or full in the sign Scorpio. It banished the terrors of the night, protected the wearer during epidemics, soothed the wild passions and gave a glimpse of the beyond. It banished the fear of death and secured a painless passing from this life to the next; it gave strength to the intellect and enabled the wearer to receive impressions from astral sources." (Kozminsky, p. 379)

Reading Excerpts

In giving the interpretations of the records as we find them here, so many unusual things appear; as the entity sees and feels those influences of the mystical force about the entity. All emblems, all languages of stones or flowers, numbers and astrological aspects appear; and the life pattern becomes beautiful, in the color—for it becomes almost as tone and voice in its response to the very nature of the entity . . .

Then, in choosing the interpretations of the records of those things that have their influence or urge—keep the topaz as a stone about thee always. Its beauty, its purity, its clarity, may bring to thee strength. For this ye have found, and will find oft needed in thy dealings with thy problems, and with thy fellow men.   2281-1, F. 32
                                                              born 5/8/08

Q-8. Is there any special color, stone or symbol that would be good for the entity to wear?
A-8. As indicated, symbols of a straight line, a T and the triangle. These are to the entity as the development or the spreading, or the closing in, as each implies.

Stones—those of the yellow tint or nature would be the better. These bring the vibrations for more harmonious influences in one who is especially influenced in Mercury, Venus and Mars. For, as each of these is indicated in the white, the red, the blue, the yellow harmonizes in same.
                                                            2648-1, F. 11
                                                              born 12/10/30

PART III
CHOOSING A GEM, STONE, OR METAL FOR ONESELF

What are truths without an ultimate regard for goodness!
Or . . . the intelligence unless to know how to choose the
Good . . .
Swedenborg
(Toksvig, 1948, p. 149)

The Problem

After studying the reading excerpts in Part II, one realizes that there are no simple rules to follow for selecting the proper gems, stones, or metals for an individual. It is insufficient, for instance, to base one's choice merely upon a birthdate* or favorite color; rather, it is necessary to understand one's "total aspect" and, as well, to know the appropriate substance which would be of most benefit to the total "vibratory pattern" or "soul force." In fact, in the absence of a contact with divine mind (or the Akashic Records), we are unable to know with certainty the stone or metal that would be most beneficial to us.

If we were capable of reading auras, this choice might be considerably easier; consider, for example, the following two excerpts:

There being, then, individuals who when wearing a fire opal would be hard individuals to deal with when it came to sex. There would be others having different effects. The same individual wearing . . . the moonstone might find that it would bring peace, harmony and those tendencies towards spiritual things. There are those to whom the bloodstone brings harmony, and less of the tendencies for anger; and so with each . . .
The auras as compared to the stones, these should work in ninety-nine percent of the conditions where these are considered as those things that work with, not against, the colors seen in the auras; that is, those which indicate the fire signs in the aura of such should never wear opals, and they will even fade flowers when worn on their bodies. 5294-1, M. 61
born 7/23/1883

---

*See calendar of birthstones, p. 45.

Q-6. Do I read auras correctly?
A-6. Not always. Study first not that which is of the physical; for, as we have indicated, auras are both physical and spiritual influences. With the subjugation of the physical the spiritual shines forth. With the exercising of the forces of the physical only these supersede; but study as in self . . . and His light will guide thee in understanding that auras are not as judgments, but so that ye may know . . .   361-4, M. 15
born 9/14/18

A Tentative Solution

In the absence of a contact with higher mind or the Akashic Records, and in the absence of an ability to read and interpret auras, one has little recourse in choosing a beneficial stone or metal but to turn to the published information that is *known* to have originated from "higher sources." From this occult knowledge one may select a stone or metal that *might* be of beneficial influence for a specific condition with which one is concerned.

By studying all that a person can about the details of the substance to be used (its proper quality, size, shape, color, mounting, and position on the body), a person might consider making a personal experiment with a given gem, stone, or metal. He could fashion and mount "his" gem (or have it done by a lapidary or jeweler to specifications) and begin wearing it according to the directions in the readings. Then, by careful self-observation (Ouspensky, 1949, p. 117), or continuous "watching himself pass by," he could become conscious of the positive, negative, or neutral effects of the stone or metal. In this way a person could—in certain cases—find a useful gem, stone, or metal for his present earthly sojourn.

An Example of "Choosing" a Stone
(Experimenting with Lapis Lazuli)

Let us say that a man recognizes a need for, and desires, strengthening influences for his body. He refers to the list on page 44 and notes that lapis lazuli was described as a stone that emitted strengthening vibrations. After studying and *understanding* the reading excerpts in Part II, under the heading "lapis lazuli," his next step involves making a list of the conditions that must be satisfied before the stone can be effectively and safely worn. He would note (from reading 691-1), for example, that the stone should be worn constantly about the body and touching the skin. The most favorable positions upon the body would be either the neck (1981-1) or about the waist

FREE CATALOG OF BOOKS
AND MEMBERSHIP ACTIVITIES

Fill-in and mail this postage-paid card today.

Please write clearly

Name: _____

Address: _____

City: _____

State/Province: _____

Postal/Zip Code: _____ Country: _____

| 110-1 |
| 11/98 |

Association for Research and Enlightenment, Inc.
215 67th Street
Virginia Beach, VA 23451-2061

For Faster Service call 1-800-723-1112
www.are-cayce.com

(3053-3). He would have to determine, by experiment, the best place for him. He would also note that the stone should be mounted between thin layers of glass (1931-2, 3416-1, 3053-3, and 1981-1), to limit the radiation emitted by the stone. (Glass acts as a trap [Price, and others, 1957, p. 322] for the electrons emitted by the stone. The streams of electrons excite molecular vibrations [Massey, 1959] and, if the electron radiation is too intense, harmful effects may be produced in groups of living cells [Tobias, 1959].)

Careful self-observation by the wearer of the gem or stone— over a period of months—would permit assessment of the strengthening influence exerted by the lapis lazuli. Similar studies could be undertaken with the other substances recommended on page 44 for strengthening influences and, theoretically, the most useful one might be found. It is to be emphasized here that experimentation with the occult properties of gems, stones, and metals must be carried out on oneself, *not on others.*

Guidance for the Experimenter

Hence the higher forces that may come through the spiritual influences in the life of the soul may be found by finding first in self, What Is *My* Ideal, and in seeking to know that the kingdom is within—and that the standards are those given by the Prince of Peace. If the associations, in seeking into psychic or soul forces in the activities, are ever surrounded by the blessings of the Christ, there may come *only* good. *Fail* not in *ever* surrounding self with that environment . . .

Study to show thyself approved unto thy God, and let thy God be *one;* not fame, not fortune, not that which is gratifying only to the desires of a body, but know that if the desire of the heart and soul is grounded in divining truth as it appears in the daily experiences of the life, self may be grounded in Truth. For, *heed* that which has been given. Make *every* act constructive, else those other influences may creep in. *Know* in whom thou has believed, knowing He is able to keep that thou committest unto Him against any environ, any condition that may arise in thine experience. For, He is in *His* holy temple; and the *temple* is within. So meet the first commands, "Thou shalt have no other gods before me," which make for the law of selfpreservation; yet if the preserving of self is at the expense of thine brother, thine neighbor, or thine own conscience, ye are setting up other gods! 440-1, M. 23
born 4/24/10

The foregoing reading provides the proper setting for experimentation. It is well to realize, also, that gems and stones are aids to soul growth only as they strengthen and guide the will of an individual. These substances do not take the place of one's will—nor do they place a person beyond the laws governing soul growth.

No shortcuts in metaphysics . . . Life is lived within self . . . Know in whom you believe and why, and then apply it in your relationship to . . . those with whom you labor . . .
Each one who has a soul has a psychic power—but remember, brother, there are no shortcuts to God! You are there—but self must be eliminated.   5392-1, M. 46
born 1/6/1898

Additional material that may aid in the preparation of an individual for experimentation that relates to meditation can be found in *A Search for God,* Books I and II. These volumes can be ordered by writing A.R.E. Press, Box 595, Virginia Beach, Virginia 23451.

Information for Experimenters

The following information is provided for readers who may be interested in studying the constructive uses of various metals, gems, and stones for meditation, the improvement of mental and physical health, or kindred purposes.

Resumé of Recommended Uses of Gems, Stones, and Metals
The gems, stones, and metals given below were recommended in Part II for the purpose indicated. It should be remembered that the same stones may affect different individuals to different degrees and that the effects themselves may be detected only with difficulty and after some time.

For Attunements:
To healing forces: amethyst, bloodstone, chrysolite, pearl
To infinity: diamond, lapis lazuli, ruby
To creative vibrations: bloodstone, pearl
For developing psychic abilities: lapis linguis
For meditation: lapis linguis
For receptiveness: agate, beryl, copper

For Specific Physical or Mental Conditions:
General protection: beryl, lapis ligurius
Protection from colds: carbon steel
Prevention of personal anger: opal, pearl, amethyst
Influencing the mental choices: bloodstone, sardonyx
Increasing abilities during exertion: agate, amethyst
Strengthening the body: lapis lazuli, bloodstone, moonstone, pearl, topaz
Gaining self-assurance: lapis lazuli

It is stressed once again that prior to using any of the stones or metals for the purposes indicated, each substance should be looked up in Part II for a thorough understanding of the conditions surrounding its usage.

Calendar of Birthstones

Though in recommending gems for individual use the Cayce readings did not seem to adhere to the traditional lists of birthstones, the reader may be interested in the calendar of stones suggested by ancient and modern sources:

Month	Ancient	Modern
January	Garnet	Garnet
February	Amethyst	Amethyst
March	Jasper	Bloodstone or Aquamarine
April	Sapphire	Diamond
May	Agate	Emerald
June	Emerald	Pearl, Moonstone or Alexandrite
July	Onyx	Ruby
August	Carnelian	Sardonyx or Peridot
September	Crysolite	Sapphire
October	Aquamarine	Opal or Tourmaline
November	Topaz	Topaz
December	Ruby	Turquoise or Zircon

Source: Retail Jewelers of America, Inc.

An interesting alternative approach to determining birthstones is outlined in S.N. Green's brief article, "Science and Birthstones," which appeared in the December, 1949, issue of *The Lapidary Journal* and was reprinted in the A.R.E. *Searchlight* of February 1, 1950. The author drew upon the work of three modern clairvoyants—Levi Downing (who transcribed *The Aquarian Gospel*), Edgar Cayce and C.W. Leadbeater—to arrive at a table of gems corresponding to the different parts of the year. The starting point was Downing's list of periods of the year and their ruling planets; each planet was then paired with the spectral color ascribed to it in the Cayce readings; finally, each color was matched with a group of related stones, taken from Leadbeater's *The Science of the Sacraments*. Eliminating the intermediate steps, we are left with the following list of gems and the dates of birth to which they correspond:

DATE OF BIRTH   *APPROPRIATE GEMS*
Jan. 19 to Feb. 17   Emerald, aquamarine, jade, malachite, peridot, amazonite, pyrite

Feb. 18 to Mar. 20	Diamond, rock crystal, white quartz, zircon, opal, magnetite
Mar. 21 to Apr. 19	Ruby, tourmaline, pyrope garnet, carnelian, carbuncle, thulite, rhodonite, red coral
Apr. 20 to May 20	Sapphire, lapis lazuli, turquoise, sodalite, benitoite, fluorite
May 21 to June 20	Topaz, citrine, steatite, cairngorm, amber, chrysotile, obsidian, jet
June 21 to July 21	Amethyst, porphyry, violan, hematite
July 22 to Aug. 22	Jasper, chalcedony, agate, serpentine, pearl, selenite, alabaster
Aug. 23 to Sept. 22	Topaz, citrine, steatite, cairngorm, amber, chrysotile, obsidian, jet
Sept. 23 to Oct. 22	Sapphire, lapis lazuli, turquoise, sodalite, benitoite, fluorite
Oct. 23 to Nov. 21	Ruby, tourmaline, pyrope garnet, carnelian, carbuncle, thulite, rhodonite, red coral
Nov. 22 to Dec. 20	Diamond, rock crystal, white quartz, zircon, opal, magnetite
Dec. 21 to Jan. 18	Emerald, aquamarine, jade, malachite, peridot, amazonite, pyrite

Appendix

REFLECTIONS OF A ROCKHOUND
by Ken Carley

I've been in the rock business since 1956 as a commercial gem and mineral dealer and as a lapidary. Over the years I've had many unusual requests both for material and special kinds of lapidary work. One of the strangest came my way back in 1960 or 1961 and little did I realize then how deep my own involvement would become. My company started receiving letters requesting pieces of different kinds of rocks. Many I had never heard of and sometimes, if the stone was small or if I had a lot of the stuff, I'd just pack it up and send it off to the writer.

In the early '60s, when the request came from a man in the south for ten or twelve different stones, I was starting to wonder who was directing these orders to me. Therefore, I sent him what I had along with the question of how he had got my name. His answer was that my company was listed in the back of a book published by an A.R.E. Press in Virginia Beach, Virginia. That didn't tell me a whole lot, but I did know Virginia Beach. As a former Navy man I had been aboard a ship or two which had steamed by the shoreline there. So I wrote him again, and this time I learned a little more. He had a booklet which he thought was written by Edgar Cayce, and its title was *Gems and Stones*. The booklet said that Edgar Cayce had recommended using stones for healing. I must admit it sounded pretty far-out to me! However, seventeen years ago being a lapidary supply dealer was considered pretty strange too.

I knew who Edgar Cayce was, because I had read by "accident" a copy of *There Is a River* and had been deeply moved by the philosophy of this man. I got a copy of *Gems and Stones* and began reading. It didn't make a lot of sense to me. I just couldn't see how these stones, some of them with really strange names, could have a healing or any other physical effect on the body. It did seem reasonable that a psychological healing might occur. It also certainly crossed my mind that some of these people might just catch the bug and become

47

rockhounds, and there is nothing that pleases a rockhound more than sharing his hobby with another person. I also knew that if the bug bites (rockhound fever?), it's usually incurable. Not long after I received the booklet I made a deal with an old tailgater from upper Michigan for a load of copper ore. Tailgating is a slang term in my business to describe an individual who makes a strike, loads up the back end of a pickup truck—usually an old beat-up truck—and drives around the country peddling his find off the tailgate. If you can remember, in the early '60s the rage in colors was swamp or olive green, and that's what the color of this material was except that there were bright specks of native copper all through it. Later, it was called Epidote and Copper, and a few other names.

It is my practice, whenever I get a new material, to work out a method of polishing so I can advise my customers and, I hope, increase my sales. I started in on this stuff in the morning and worked on it most of the day. My first discovery was that it was so loaded with copper that my diamond saws would bind up and wouldn't cut. I had to spend a lot of time dressing the blades. By late in the morning I had a heck of a headache. At first I thought it was a sinus headache and took some medicine, but it didn't go away. It felt like somebody was hitting me in the center of my forehead with a broom handle. There was lots of pressure and it sure did smart!

I could hardly see—let alone work—so I left the shop and was thinking about going home. By then, though, my headache started to ease off, so I went to dinner instead. In the afternoon I got back to working on the stuff, and just about the time I was beginning to get a polish, I became aware of what felt like cobwebs on my forehead, and a bad taste in my mouth. I finished up for the day and went home feeling kind of weird. I remember telling my wife that I'd had a late customer and that I had known everything he was going to say and some of the things he didn't say—like he was talking inside my head. I experienced about the same thing with her. (Not all of what she was saying inside my head, however, was kind.)

That night, lying in bed trying to sort through the day's happenings, I only knew I hadn't been out in the sun too long, and I couldn't remember that anybody had hit me on the head with a rock. Then, all of a sudden, the pieces of the puzzling day started falling into place. Whatever had happened to me had something to do with that rock. Wow! It really blew my mind.

The moral of this story: keep an open mind. If it doesn't fit right now into what you think you know, just put it on a shelf for awhile. Let it be. (It's taken a lot of years and experience for me to come up with that nugget of wisdom—and a rather constant diet of crow!)

Ever since that experience with the olive green stone, I've been pretty much open to the influences of copper material, and also to the somewhat subdued effects of aluminum.

But there's more to the story. I struggled with the concepts in the *Gems* booklet involving the mechanism of influence in these materials. I struggled with the wording of the Cayce readings, the depth of ideas. I felt like an ant trying to move a mountain, pushing one grain of sand at a time.

Maybe the start of wisdom is the realization of how little one really knows about a subject. I could hardly believe that only a short time before I had thought I was an expert!

In the past twelve or thirteen years I've moved a lot of sand. Every time I've found a keystone, a lot more sand fell into the hole. Sometimes I've felt like chucking the whole thing. I've wanted to find a smaller mountain or just let it be. But I guess those ways won't work for me. There is something inside me that just won't let me let go.

Perhaps it is coming into the realization of the reality of the oneness which is all. Maybe if, like my brother, I can go beyond the intellect, reach the simplicity of the spheres and come into the all knowledge, all wisdom, all love, all understanding of the universal consciousness we call God . . . but I'm not there yet! Since the journey of a thousand miles starts with the first step, let me step forth!

As I see it: Our bodies, like the universe, are atomic in nature. Outside stimuli such as rocks and gems create an electromagnetic influence which affects man's body. There is a word picture which has helped me understand this. Imagine, if you can, an angel with a harp sending forth a tone which, for our example, is the tone of creation. Now imagine a tuning fork which represents a gem. The elements of the body can be thought of as many tiny tuning forks. As the word or tone of creation is sounded, the gem—the larger tuning fork—starts to vibrate at a certain frequency. The tiny tuning forks of the body which are set at that frequency also start vibrating. When the gem tuning fork is near the body, the body's tuning forks which are set at the same frequency (those which are "in sympathy") respond to the stimulus and increase their vibration.

In giving that which may be helpful it is necessary, for this mind or body seeking same, that there be rather the analysis of the composition of the stones as related to their vibrations—as relate then to a human body, see?

Either of these show a variation of their composition; as to the elements of those influences that make for vibrations in the ether as related to that which may be effective in drawing to or disseminating from—through, of course, the vibrations being those that are of the positive and negative natures in the very stone itself—making for, then, the analysis; knowing same by what is called the constituents of it, through the mineralogy, the activity through those channels themselves. We would then find that the one that is the nearer in accord to the vibrations of the body that may use same would be the more effective with *that* particular body. Yet the very *nature* of the thing makes it effective with any—*any*—human body, you see; but the more effective with one that is more in accord, or whose positive and negative vibrations are according with the stone itself, see? for it throws off as well as draws in, you see, through the positive-negative vibration. This assists, then, in the unison as a relationship. This is as a comparison— don't confuse it and say that it is electricity; it is electrical, of course, in its vibration, but as the stone in its vibration is then in sympathy with a body that is also sympathetic—or may be said to be *sensitive*—it assists in "stepping up" the sensitiveness of the body as would the electrical vibration in an alternating force step up by the addition of influences or forces of electrical vibration being thrown off from other channels in making it more powerful. See? Towards what? Towards the effectiveness in its sensitiveness (that is, the body) as to what it may be seeking. Hence, as given of old, use such for the abilities to become more of all those influences called in the present psychic, clairaudient, or any of those vibrations that build up or "step up" a body. Also effective, of course, in bringing to the body the abilities to become more effective in giving out of itself for activity in any of these various directions.   440-18

We can never assume that once we are in possession of a gem, a metal, or a rock we have a direct pipeline to Heaven and may do as we please. The readings lay it right on the line. It is always our own responsibility to use these influences correctly if we want to find the Christ way for our lives.

But, as the body should comprehend in regard to all such influences, it is as to what the body does about same; not that it relies upon such, but knowing that such influences aid in increasing the ability or efficiency in the periods of exertion or activity, use them rather as stepping-stones and not those things upon which the activities in a mental and spiritual plane would be builded. They are step stones rather than foundations, then, in the experience.   500-1

Q-2. How can I use the ... vibrations from metal, from stones which influence me, to advantage in my present life?
A-2. As these are but lights, but signs in thine experience; they are as but a candle that one stumbles not in the dark. But worship *not* the light of the candle; rather that to which it may guide thee in thy service.

So whether [thou art guided] from the vibrations of numbers, of metals, of stones, these are merely to become the necessary influences to make thee in attune, one with the Creative Forces; just as the pitch of a song of praise is not the song nor the message therein, but is a helpmeet for those that would find strength in the service of the Lord. So, use them to attune self. How, ye ask? As ye apply, ye are given the next step.

Q-3. Should I carry these stones on my person, and how may I know through meditation the message they would give me?

A-3. If necessary. And how may ye know? These do not give the messages! They only attune self so that the Christ Consciousness may give the message! Listen to no message of a stone, of a number, even of a star; for they are but servants of the Lord and Master of all—even as thou! 767-2

So far as I know, there are about ninety readings which deal either directly or indirectly with gems, stones and metals. It seems to me that those materials which are referred to several times have greater universal significance and usefulness than those referred to only once. I believe there are certain criteria interwoven throughout the language of the readings which may be used to identify other materials which might be better suited for an individual than those specifically mentioned. While each of these readings was given for an individual, and therefore is specific for that person, there seems also to be a tie-in with regard to an exact body position. Does this body position correspond to a physiological center, or is it a psychological one? If physiological, how does it relate to the ductless glands, the endocrine centers, the concept of the "Golden Man"?

Before a hypothesis can be stated, the known facts must be established. In this case, the relevant readings must be identified and correlated. Since accepting the "opportunity" for such a research, I've been through those ninety readings well over a dozen times. I still have far more questions than answers. I have observed, however, that many little tidbits in the readings open up whole new meanings for me. My plans for the future include these efforts:

1. Show which materials were suggested most often and deal with them in that order.

2. Use all the readings where practical and possible. (This might present some problem. Lapis Lazuli, for example, has been referred to specifically seventeen times, in readings for fifteen different persons.)

3. Where the names of materials are different from those now in common usage, the reader will be given his choice, based on:

    a. data suggested in the readings

    b. known chemical, mineralogical and geological facts

c. whatever historical and/or occult uses may be found for a given material

d. experimental findings of a meditation workshop

e. my own experience as a lapidary (for whatever it is worth) and those effects which I have noted occurring in me.

4. Attempt to establish criteria, based on the readings, for aiding the seeker to determine which materials are best suited to that individual, and suggest other materials not mentioned in the readings.

5. Try to discover if there is a connection between suggested body positions and the ductless glands.

6. Establish the intended uses for these materials.

7. Show the interrelationship between color and other forms of vibration as mentioned in the readings.

My business for the past seventeen years has been on the rocks, sometimes in more ways than one. I've had an "opportunity" to explore this vast subject. I no longer claim to be an expert, and what I think I know today may change by tomorrow. I am only trying to use what is at hand.

There are some inherent faults in a chart such as the following one. I do not know positively that only eighty-nine readings are involved. There could be more than one material referred to as Lapis Lazuli. It is also not too clear in the readings whether Lapis refers to Lapis Lingua or Lapis Lazuli, or some other material. Therefore, I listed it separately. The Scarab, the Maltese Cross and the Combination Stone made from Soya Bean were placed on the list as items of general interest only. The list does suggest reasonable doubt as to the validity of ascribing curative powers to carbon steel.

The first column designates the number of different entity readings recommending a particular material. For example, in the 440 series there are five readings dealing with "lapis"; in this column these five readings are shown as one. Column 2 lists the total number of readings dealing with a particular recommended material, and includes follow-up readings. Column 3 is included because previous writers have pointed to some significance about materials "mentioned" in the readings. I quite frankly question this, but feel it is important to note and let the reader draw his/her own conclusion. (Example: reading 1931-1 recommended Lapis Ligurius. "This is the *green stone,* you see—the *crystallization of copper* and those influences that are creative within themselves . . . Hence the radial activity of *radium,* as well as the strengthening influences of *gold,* the stabilizing influences of *silver* . . ." Each of the italicized materials is shown in this column and the number indicated shows how often these materials were thus "mentioned" in other readings.)

Material	Number of Times Specifically Recommended	Total Number of Readings Recommending and/or Explaining	Number of Times "Mentioned" in Other Readings
Lapis Lazuli	14	16	1
Pearl	11	11	1
Pearl/Moonstone	2	2	
Pearl/Jade	1	1	
Ruby	9	9	1
Bloodstone	7	7	3
Bloodstone/Lapis Lazuli	1	1	
Moonstone	5	5	1
Lapis	3	8	1*
Opal	6	6	2
Amethyst	5	5	
Coral	5	5	1
Agate	4	4	
Lapis Ligurius	1	2	
Lapis Lingua	1	2	1
Lapis Linguis	3	4	
Lapis Languis	1	1	
Ruby/Onyx	1	1	
Crystal or White Stone	3	3	1
Beryl	3	3	1
Blue Stone	3	3	
Diamonds	3	3	3
Jade	1	1	
Onyx	1	1	
Sardonyx	1	1	
Sardius	1	1	
Carbon	1	1	
Chalcedony	1	1	
Chrysolite	1	1	1
Blue-Green Chalcedony	1	1	1*
Green Stone			1
Topaz	1	1	
Yellow Tint	1	1	
Zinc	1	1	
Carbon Steel	1	1	
Platinum	2	2	
Gold	2	2	5
White gold			1
Silver	1	1	3
Copper	6	6	3
Azurite			1
Coal			1
Ivory			1
Emerald			2
Stellyte			1
Radium			1
Uranium			1
Combination of stone made from Soya Bean			1

*There is a letter on record written to [440] about an experience Edgar Cayce had with [813], suggesting a tie with blue-green chalcedony and "lapis."

Material	Number of Times Specifically Recommended	Total Number of Readings Recommending and/or Explaining	Number of Times "Mentioned" in Other Readings
Turquoise Blue			1
Pigeon-Blood Ruby			1
Scarab			2
Maltese Cross			2

THE STONES OF EGYPT
by Ken Carley

Ever since I can remember, I have been fascinated by Egypt and its ancient cultures. The numerous Edgar Cayce readings on Egypt and their frequent recommendations that gems and stones be used for healing purposes suggest a strong tie with the reports of archaeologists.

In Doris Hodges' *Healing Stones,* Fay Clark speculates that the Atlanteans brought the use of stones for occult and healing purposes, and there is evidence that the ancient Egyptians had knowledge of the stones' chemical composition and their uses. The Eber Papyrus recommends lapis lazuli as an ingredient for eye salves and hematite (an iron oxide) for checking hemorrhages and reducing inflammation.

It might also be noted that the Egyptians were greatly afraid of the "dark forces" and spent a good deal of time and effort in protecting themselves from their influences. According to G.F. Kunz in *The Curious Lore of Precious Stones,* there is, in the Munch Collection at the Metropolitan Museum of Art in New York, a piece of limestone, the hieroglyphs on which state in the cursive Egyptian of 1600 B.C., that lapis lazuli was used by the wealthy (and hematite by those of limited means) for the treatment of hysteria. Reading 1931-1 says that lapis ligurius (probably malachite) would act as "a *protective* influence."

In their manufacture of jewelry and ornaments the ancient Egyptians also used many stones which, today, would be considered of low commercial value. The Egyptian craftsmen, with very few exceptions, used stones which were available locally. Pliny mentions about thirty different kinds of precious stones which would be found in Egypt or Ethiopia. Because he used names whose meaning has been lost to time, very few of them can be identified. However, archaeological investigation indicates that the principal stones were agate, amethyst, beryl, calcite, carnelian, chalcedony, coral, feldspar, garnet, hematite, jade, jadeite, jasper, lapis lazuli, malachite, olivine, onyx, pearl, peridot, rock crystal, sard, sardonyx, and turquoise.[1]

The Cayce readings describe a prehistoric King Araaraat who drew the races together and developed their abilities. Under his leadership the rich material resources of the land were discovered. Mines were opened at Ophir (later called Kadesh) in Persia, in Abyssinia and in other areas of the upper Nile. There was mining of such diverse precious stones as onyx, beryl, sardius, diamond, amethyst, and opal. Pearls were taken from the sea near what is now Madagascar. Stone cutting and polishing was encouraged as a major craft. From other mines about the country iron, lead, zinc, tin, copper, silver, and gold were produced. Much jewelry was made.

Thanks to the Egyptian habit of recording every detail, there are many Egyptian writings which have been carefully preserved and are in collections in the great museums of the world. These writings tell us about the uses to which precious stones were put throughout pre-dynastic as well as later dynastic periods. Gemstones were often acceptable as tribute and were always among the more important spoils of war.[2]

It is interesting that the Cayce readings and some of the surviving Egyptian writings speak of diamonds, opals, sapphires, and rubies while the archaeologists have stated that these particular stones were not known to the ancient Egyptian.[3] Possibly, they are both right. The confusion may be due to the changes of names. Perhaps the "diamond" of the ancients and of the readings was rock crystal, yet the readings refer to both. The sapphire is another puzzler and to what stone this name was given is not certain. For some, including Pliny, it seems to be confused with lapis lazuli. For others, sapphires seem confused with turquoise and the hyacinth.[4] Perhaps with time and new discoveries, the Cayce readings and the archaeologists will agree.

At the time of their use, the stones of ancient Egypt were costly and highly prized. The most commonly used materials were the silica-based carnelian onyx, sardonyx and agate. Today, these are usually grouped together as agate which, in turn, is a sub-variety of chalcedony.

Agate beads, as well as onyx, have been found in predynastic graves. They were also used to a limited extent in jewelry of the early dynastic periods. Carnelian is found in the form of pebbles in the eastern desert of Egypt where it occurs in abundance. It had very early use in the pre-dynastic era as beads and amulets. In later times, it was used for inlays on jewelry and sarcophagi and on various pieces of furniture. The earliest use of sardonyx, according to the archaeologists, was in the 22nd Dynasty, and the principal use of agate, sardonyx, and onyx was in the creation of jars or canopic vessels. This is evidenced by the discovery of such vessels in ancient tombs.

> [In Egypt] the entity gained in abilities to give to others that understanding as attained from the builders and from those who wrought in fine metals, those who had the understandings of precious stones and their settings, and their colors, and their vibrations, as gave for the influences in peoples. In this the entity gained, and the stones the entity should have about same, is the sardius—for this gives for an influence as may be best made in the entity's influence to understand those laws as apply to man's relationships to the higher forces.   1714-1

Amethyst was used primarily in necklaces. However, the gem was also used in bracelets, beads, amulets, and scarabs. Its major use came during the period of the Middle Kingdom, continuing until the Roman times. Old amethyst workings have been discovered about 40 miles northwest of the original Temple of Abu Simbel and other workings 20 miles southeast of Aswan. Most of the Egyptian deposits and the artifacts found there are rather pale, but two very fine amethyst scarabs were found in the tomb of Tutankhamen. It may be worth noting that some Brazilian amethyst specimens known today seem to have a tendency to become pale after long periods of exposure to sunlight.

The Rubric of Chapter CXL of the Egyptian *Book of the Dead,* to be recited during the longest day of the Egyptian year, was repeated over two Udjat amulets, one of them to be made of lapis lazuli and the other, of amethyst or carnelian.[5]

The use of natural resins and amber reach as far back in Egyptian history as the pre-dynastic periods. Some of these resins have proved difficult to identify. Discovered in the tomb of Tutankhamen were a double ring, a variety of beads and scarabs, a unique hair ring, and a pair of earrings, all of which were made of a dark red resin of unknown organic origin.[6] Perhaps other objects identified earlier by archaeologists will prove, through further investigation, to be incorrectly identified.

Extensive old workings of the mineral, beryl, occur in the Sikait-Zubara region of the Red Sea hills. These workings could have been the source of these materials for the Egyptians. Some authorities, however, think they are more likely of Greco-Roman origin. The materials from these mines are always transparent or translucent—never opaque. Many stones of such good quality as to be called emerald have been taken from this deposit.[7] Most of these gems are full of flaws, however, and by our standards unfit for jewelry. Most of the crystals are pale or whitish green. Prized for their hexagonal shape, the early working of these gems was in the form of beads and pendants. It was late in the dynastic periods before the Egyptians learned to cut the stone satisfactorily. The scarcity of beryl artifacts in the tombs indicates its limited use in pre-dynastic times. One large uncut emerald was taken, however, from a pre-dynastic grave at Kubanieh.

> ... we find [the entity] in that land known as the Egyptian ... then in the household of the priest, and of those that waited on the companion of the priest. In the name Is-Eli. In this experience the entity rose to power, position, place, fame, through the experiences in that period, as related to the various manners of expression of praise in music, in art, and *especially* in that of placing of stones. In the present, the innate desire to feel precious stones, to compare same, to watch the change in the color in same, is seen from *this* experience. These will make for much *judgment* to the entity, and the beryl and scarab should be a portion of the entity's dress, *ever;* either worn as the amulet, the ring, or such, will make for a safety in the entity's present experience. 1719-1

Calcite, known in Egypt as alabaster, is found in abundance in that country's eastern desert. The pure, transparent variety is termed Iceland spar, and this is the variety which exhibits a double reflective ability. It was used in flat cleavage pieces, as inlay for jewelry and furniture. Dating from about the 6th Dynasty on, it seems to have been used in cylindrical seals, and several varieties of these have been found in almost all of the more important dynastic tombs.

A number of forms of carnelian were used. The darker, almost black varieties are called sard and were used, to a small extent, in pre-dynastic times. Yellow carnelian was used occasionally for beads. Other forms of agate—more correctly called banded chalcedony—occur commonly in Egypt. They are usually grayish white but, due to depth or cutting technique, often display a bluish tint. They were used for beads, pendants, and scarabs.

Another form of chalcedony, chrysophrase—colored apple green by nickel in silica—has been found in beads of pre-dynastic periods. There are several excellent examples of these in the Berlin Museum.

Carnelian was "called a 'blood stone' because it acted on the blood, and prevented it from rising in excess to the head."[8] There is much confusion about the material, bloodstone, and my attempts to determine what the material really is have resulted in a number of headaches. Hematite has been called bloodstone because it streaks a red oxide or, when scratched, shows red dust. Jasper, also, has been connected with the term. Jasper is an impure, opaque, and very compact form of silica. It occurs in a variety of colors, all of them due to the presence of iron. Jasper, in green, brown, black, yellow, and other colors, is common in Egypt, and all colors were used by the ancients. Red was most often used for amulets and inlay, and a few scarabs have been discovered. Green jasper was highly prized and was used from earliest times. A large vein of green jasper has been discovered; it is sometimes flecked with red spots. This vein shows evidence of early workings located in the eastern desert. Today, bloodstone (or heliotrope) is described as dark green chalcedony with small spots or flecks of red jasper. Yet the Cayce readings say:

Have about the entity stones that are red; as the bloodstone, the ruby, or everything of that nature. **1616-1**

The name, bloodstone, is also applied to red coral, red agate, red marble, red jasper, carnelian, and heliotrope.[9]

Hence the bloodstone or the ruby is well to ever be about the entity. **1770-2**

Keep not as a charm, but as the influences that may bring the greater force about the body, the moonstone or the bloodstone as the ornaments about the body; but those that will be found (that are akin to these) in the turquoise blue and the pigeon-blood ruby. **608-7**

Since the Egyptians borrowed the Zodiac from the Greeks,[10] there may be another factor which points toward red as the color of bloodstone. Mars, the "red planet," is the planet of Aries, and the bloodstone is the Arian birthstone. The influence of Mars is said to incite man to mighty deeds, to perform works of valor which often result in the shedding of blood. The ancient astrologers believed that precious and semi-precious stones were bearers of the influences of the stars and planets. They associated Mars with red stones: ruby, hematite, jasper, and bloodstone.[11]

Although coral comes in white, red, and black varieties, only white and red appear in Egyptian jewelry.[12] White coral artifacts such as necklaces and bracelets from the 19th Dynasty and later have been found. Also found were two forms of red coral, solid and branching, the latter being more highly valued and used in amulets, beads, and pendants. Two other forms of coral are known to have had limited use—pipe coral and fossil coral. Outcroppings of fossil deposits have been found in the western desert.

The Cayce readings which refer to coral do not mention Egypt, but the following excerpt suggests some reasons that coral was used as an amulet:

Yet there are those things that make for harmony in their relationships as one to another, as do the turmoils of the mother-water that brings forth in its activity about the earth those tiny creatures that in their beginning make for the establishing of that which is the foundation of much of these in materiality. Hence the red, the deep red coral, upon thine flesh, will bring quietness in those turmoils that have arisen within the inner self . . .   694-2

That feldspar, in the form of Amazonite or Amazon stone, was used for beads has been reported from the earliest periods. It is usually pale green in color. Very early and extensive workings have been found in the Eghei mountains. The green feldspar has often been confused, by archaeologists, with other green stones such as emerald and beryl.

The most frequently found iron artifacts of the Middle Kingdom appear to be small amulets made of magnetic iron or magnetite.[13] Hematite, black with metallic luster, was used for beads, and might have come from the eastern desert.

Some artifacts have been identified as jade or jadeite. However, because their current owners are unwilling to allow these pieces to be tested, there may be a question as to their exact composition. There are no known deposits of jade or jadeite in or around Egypt.

The next material, lapis lazuli, is perhaps the most mystifying of any of the stones mentioned in the Cayce readings. It was the material held in highest regard by the Egyptians. Many of the early cultures—Chinese, Tibetan, Persian, Indian, etc.—desired and sought after lapis lazuli. Artifacts from the earliest Egyptian periods verify the use of this gem. It found its way into the most beautiful, most loved, and best designed pieces of Egyptian work. To understand the love and regard the ancient peoples of Egypt had for this material, one should read a passage in the Egyptian Book of the Dead, Chapter XV (A Hymn to Ra, The Sun God) which describes Ra rising in the eastern heaven. Heaven is represented by lapis lazuli.

Lapis lazuli is actually an aggregate of several minerals. It is formed through metamorphic action of a magma body on a sedimentary deposit of limestone. Generally, the chemical composition of this gem material is a combination of silicates of sodium and aluminum with some necessary calcium, chlorine, and sulfur. It is relatively soft, having a hardness of 5 to 5.5 on the Mohs scale. It has a granular texture, is opaque, and its polished surfaces show a waxy luster. Its color range includes gray-blue, azure-blue and Berlin-blue. Sometimes it contains specks of "gold" (iron pyrite) against a rich deep-blue background. Pliny called it "sapphirus," but the name, lapis lazuli, now often shortened to lapis, was given to the material in the Middle Ages. It comes from the Latin word meaning "stone" and an Arabic word meaning "blue."[14]

While there have been statements that lapis lazuli does occur in Egypt, no evidence is ever cited. As far as is presently known, no deposits nor old workings have been found. The abundant usage of lapis for beads, amulets, scarabs, inlays, and a great variety of small objects, from the earliest pre-dynastic periods to the time of the Roman conquests, would seem to indicate otherwise. It is just one more mystery surrounding this beautiful gem.

The Cayce readings have quite a bit to say about lapis. In fact, it was recommended more often in the readings than any other gem.

For the entity should ever wear about the body the lapis lazuli or the lapis linguis; for these will bring strength to the body through those vibrations that are brought or built in the innate experience of the entity from its sojourn in the Egyptian land. **691-1**

The real puzzle occurs in the readings which follow:

The lapis lazuli stone would be well to wear about the body. This is as a chrysalis, to be sure, of copper . . . **880-2**

. . . the lapis or copper in its *elemental* form . . . **1580-1**

. . . it would be very helpful for the entity to wear upon the body a piece of stone that is of the lapis lazuli variety, but the essence or fusion of copper . . . **1651-2**

In reading after reading the statement was made that lapis, or lapis lazuli, was composed of copper. The material now known as lapis lazuli is a silicate of sodium and aluminum! No copper is present, or if it does occur, there are only trace amounts. Is this an error which occurs in the Cayce readings? Is the lapis lazuli of the readings a different material than that which is now known as lapis lazuli?

One must wonder about this discrepancy because it appears in all the readings which deal with lapis and lapis lazuli. Is this, then, part of that fifteen percent margin of error referred to in *The Outer Limits of Edgar Cayce's Power*,[15] or did the readings reveal something which has yet to be recognized by "science"?

In the 440 series, a number of readings were given regarding lapis and lapis lingua. The readings which supposedly tie up lapis lingua with azurite say:

[Suggestion given E.C.] You will have before you the body and inquiring mind of [440]... also the information given this entity through this channel in a recent series of readings, together with his endeavors to follow out some of the suggestions given him, to seek the lapis lingua in the Museum of Natural History in New York. You will answer the questions which he has submitted.

[E.C.]... In the seeking, as was given in the information, the lapis—not lapis lingua, because that is different but of the same formation, or comes from the same formation—but the lapis is there, in the hall—north side—front of the north window, in the mineral division here—large blue stone. It weighs nearly a ton and has many facets, in the manner in which it was removed from the mines; is from Arizona, and the color necessary for use as instructed—may be seen by stooping below or getting the light through a portion of the upper part, though—to be sure—it's very much thicker than would be necessary for use. It's there! Not lapis linguis, but *lapis!*

440-9

Q-6. This stone contains malachite and azurite. Is the lapis linguis either of these?
A-6. The azurite. 440-11

In the American Museum of Natural History in New York there is a huge block of azurite ore. It is about four feet in each of six directions and is riddled with vugs (holes) lined with botryoidal and crystalized azurite. It came from Bisbee, Arizona.[16]

We know the Egyptians were mining copper; malachite, an oxide of copper, is in evidence in the artifacts. In the copper deposits of southwestern United States (and generally), malachite and azurite occur together. Although it occurs with malachite, alters to it, and has many of the same chemical properties, azurite nevertheless presents as striking a color contrast as can be imagined. Its azure-blue color, from which the name is derived, is as brilliant as the green of malachite.[17]

I believe there is reason to question the identification of the blue gem artifacts from the Egyptian pre-dynastic and later periods as lapis lazuli. There are enough unresolved mysteries concerning lapis to re-study the entire subject. I hope to study it more thoroughly at a later time.

As stated earlier, malachite is found in Egyptian artifacts and, like other materials, has been confused with other green stones. It occurs in both the Sinai and the eastern deserts. Old workings indicate that the Egyptians worked both areas. Malachite was primarily used in the form of a cosmetic, as an eye paint. Only rarely was this gem used in inlay or jewelry.[18] It is a very common artifact from the early and middle periods, and there are some rough beads from pre-dynastic times worked into pieces such as amulets. It was often shaped into insects or animal forms. Occasionally it appears in small oval plaques of a religious nature.

The archaeologists tell us that while the Egyptians used large quantities of mother-of-pearl and mollusk shells from the coastal waters of the Red Sea, pearls were never used extensively by the Egyptians! Of course, "not all crows are black," if there is one exception. One such exception appears in the button pearls found in the tomb of Queen Ahhotpe of the beginning of the 18th Dynasty.[19]

Olivine is scattered throughout Egypt. It is translucent to transparent, olive-green, and has an olive-oil luster. In the Bible, Job praised the value of wisdom and said, "The topaz of Ethiopia shall not equal it." (Job 28:19) This material we know as peridot, the gem variety of the mineral olivine. Large amounts of olivine were used early as beads, but it was in the tombs of the 18th Dynasty that gem peridot was discovered. This by no means precludes earlier knowledge or use of the material.

There is an old legend about a triangular-shaped island, Topazios, in the Red Sea. It is thought that the word topaz is derived from this name. This island, now called St. John's, or Zeberged, is located 34 miles off the coast of Egypt. The topaz or, as we know it, peridot, was discovered in the stone crevices of the island.[20] The Crusaders brought many of these fine stones to Europe thinking them to be emeralds. Crysolite, meaning "golden stone," is the term given the varieties of olivine which are yellowish or yellowish-green. Chemically, olivine is a silicate of magnesium and iron. Mineral olivine also occurs in meteorites. These strange celestial visitors are thought to have been the source of the unusual silica glass found in the tombs of the Middle Kingdom and later. Large lumps of this material have been discovered southwest of the sand sea in the Libyan desert. Its color is pale greenish-yellow, and better pieces are quite clear and transparent.

An incorrect translation of Egyptian writing is believed to account for the fact that turquoise has been confused with malachite; it is possible that many of the early archaeologists made some errors in attempting to classify gems by their colors. Turquoise was used abundantly by the ancient craftsmen and examples have been found from the 4th Dynasty, in the tomb of Hetepheres at Giza, and later.[21] Most Egyptian turquoise has a green color, and this would help explain how it could have been incorrectly identified. It was used mainly as inlay and, to some extent, as scarabs. It is found as veins in the sandstone outcrops at Wadi Magharah in the Sinai Peninsula. Deposits and workings are suspected in other areas because of the coloration of some artifacts. Turquoise is usually blue, green, or any combination of these two colors. I have seen specimens of "turq" which were midnight or navy blue and others which look like jade. Chemically, the mineral may be loosely defined as a hydrous phosphite of aluminum and copper with traces of iron. It is found most often in the oxide level in copper deposits.

Turquoise, as such, is not referred to in the Cayce readings. However, with further study, it might be shown as a possible "lapis" material.

Quartz, in crystalline form, is commonly referred to as rock crystal. When clear, it was highly regarded by ancient peoples, and when found in large pieces, was cut into objects of great beauty and high esthetic quality.[22] It was found throughout Egypt, in small quantities, as clear crystal. In an old working west of Abu Simbel, quartz of good quality is still found. The counterfeiting of other gem materials by the use of clear quartz (and later, glazes and ceramic work) seems to have started around the 18th Dynasty. Perhaps this would indicate a loss of earlier knowledge concerning the use of gems, the decay of ancient wisdom, or it may have been merely an advance in technology.

Clear quartz has long been identified with magic and magical rites. It is most often associated with crystal gazing. In Egypt it is found in sarcophagi and as the eyes in statues. In the following reading it is interesting to note the suggestion to "image" or "picturize."

Well to develop, then, the imaginative forces; but picturize or visualize for the entity all those influences or forces *in* the developing of such in the experience of this entity . . .
In stones—the whiter, the more crystal the better. 1775-1

Other uses of quartz included the making of small vases.

From the recorded information, it would seem that the ancient Egyptian incorporated a great deal of esoteric knowledge in the production of his arts and crafts by the use of "home" (locally found) materials. (These materials may have been used for the purpose of polarizing the body.) On a number of occasions, the Cayce readings suggested the use of locally grown foods, or medicines, to help the body adjust to a particular region, and local stones may have similar effects. The stones suggested by the readings can, for the most part, be found in North America. As this study shows, they are also found in Egypt.

REFERENCES

1. Lucas, A., ed., *Ancient Egyptian Materials and Industries*, p. 386
2. Moriarty, J.R., "Precious Gems in Ancient Egypt," *Lapidary Journal*, September 1970, p. 794
3. Petrie, W.M.F., *Prehistoric Egypt*, p. 44; Ball, S.H., *A Roman Book on Precious Stones*, pp. 217-221
4. Budge, E.A.W., *Amulets and Talismans*, p. 323
5. Ibid, p. 142
6. Carter, H., and A.C. Mace, *Tomb of Tut-Ankh-Amen*, p. 84
7. Hume, W.F., *Geology of Egypt*, p. 859
8. Budge, p. 310
9. Ibid, p. 314
10. Ibid, p. 411
11. Ibid, p. 423
12. Moriarty, p. 797
13. Petrie, p. 43
14. Pearl, R.M., *Popular Gemology*, p. 182
15. Cayce, Edgar Evans, and Hugh Lynn Cayce, *The Outer Limits of Edgar Cayce's Power*, p. 24
16. Jones, R.W., "Arizona Minerals in Retrospect," *Lapidary Journal*, April 1973, p. 132
17. Pearl, pp. 170-171
18. Moriarty, p. 802
19. Lucas, p. 402
20. Pearl, p. 138
21. Moriarty, p. 802
22. Ibid, p. 802

BIBLIOGRAPHY

Ball, S.H., *A Roman Book on Precious Stones*, Gemological Institute of America, Los Angeles, Ca., 1964

Budge, E.A.W., *Amulets and Talismans*, University Books, New Hyde Park, N.Y., 1961

Budge, E.A.W., *The Egyptian Book of the Dead*, University Books, New Hyde Park, N.Y., 1960

Carter, H., and A.C. Mace, *Tomb of Tut-Ankh-Amen*, 3 vols., Cooper Square Publishers, New York, 1954

Hodges, D.M., *Healing Stones*, Pyramid Publishers of Iowa, Hiawatha, Iowa, 1961

Hume, W.F., *Geology of Egypt*, Government Press, Cairo, 1925

Jones, R.W., "Arizona Minerals in Retrospect," *Lapidary Journal*, April 1973

Kunz, G.F., *The Curious Lore of Precious Stones*, Dover Publications, New York, 1971

Lucas, A., ed., *Ancient Egyptian Materials and Industries*, 4th ed. rev. by J.R. Harris, St. Martin's Press, New York, 1962

Moriarty, J.R., "Precious Gems in Ancient Egypt," *Lapidary Journal*, September 1970

Pearl, R.M., *Popular Gemology*, Science Editions, John Wiley & Sons, New York, 1965

Petrie, W.M.F., *Historical Scarabs*, D. Nutt, London, 1889

Petrie, W.M.F., *Prehistoric Egypt*, British School of Archaeology in Egypt, London, 1920

LAPIS LAZULI
by Ken Carley

The most frequently mentioned gem material in the Cayce readings seems, actually, to exist in a variety of forms. Perhaps a study of this material can best be made by taking the readings apart, extracting descriptions of the materials not now known, and applying them to materials we do know. I must confess my surprise at finding so much detailed information in the readings. The excerpts used here are by no means all possible ones on the subject, but they seem representative and were selected to present a wide span of physical qualities without too much duplication. Conclusions concerning them are left to you.

Questions have been raised about lapis, lapis lazuli, lapis linguis, and lapis ligurius, as to whether there are really five materials or only three. According to the readings there are three basic stones associated, through mineral content, with each other. The readings indicate what some of their different effects may be. A complete listing of all readings consulted is included for your own further research. The personal experiences presented here are offered with the hope that they may help give deeper insight into the nature of these stones.

Evidently, these stones have definite influences on one's body. Lapis lazuli helps to develop innate psychic abilities and to increase sensitivity (440-3, 440-9). Its high electrical vibration may give strength and aid to an individual (691-1, 813-1, 816-3). It helps one create a better relationship between the mental and spiritual selves; it helps one to place material things in their proper perspective (880-2, 1580-1, 1651-2). It also brings "intenseness, the abilities to loose emotions through the very centers of the body . . . " (1580-1), and brings life and vitality into manifestation through healing (2282-1, 2132-1, 1931-4 letter, 1651-2, 1580-1).

It has often puzzled me that Cayce used names which are foreign to present usage, or names which we recognize but which appear to refer to other materials. Why use the name lapis lazuli, and then describe known characteristics of copper?

Were these names deliberately used to disguise the gem, to protect its use for those of sincere heart? There is value in seeking, because the end result is a far greater understanding of ourselves. One learns early in the study of the "mysteries" the awesome responsibility of possessing knowledge. The more knowledge one acquires, the more responsibility one has for its use. Cayce has said that knowledge not used is sin. I like the definition of sin as "missing the mark."

I cannot approach this subject without realizing my responsibility for the right use of what I have learned. If I allow any special knowledge of stones to remain hidden and do not attempt to "lift the veil," I feel that I would be missing the mark. I believe the time is at hand to make known, as best we can, what is disguised—to present all aids for finding the Christ-way.

As these are but lights, but signs in thine experience, they are as but a candle that one stumbles not in the dark. But worship *not* the light of the candle; rather that to which it may guide thee in thy service. So, whether [thou art guided] from the vibrations of numbers, of metals, of stones, these are merely to become the necessary influences to make thee in attune, one with the Creative Forces; just as the pitch of a song of praise is not the song nor the message therein, but is a helpmeet for those that would find strength in the service of the Lord. So, use them to attune self. How, ye ask? As ye apply, ye are given the next step.   707-2

Lapis lazuli is a rock consisting of an aggregate of several minerals. Any given specimens will show differences in exact mineral content. Lapis lazuli is formed through the metamorphic action of a magma body (igneous) on impure limestone. Its major mineral content is restricted to the blue minerals, all of them members of the feldspathoid group. Generally, its chemical composition consists of silicates of sodium and aluminum, with some necessary calcium, chlorine and sulfur. It has a moderate hardness, ranging from 5 to 5.5 on the Mohs scale.

Its name, now often shortened to "lapis," was given to this gem material in the Middle Ages. It comes partly from the Latin word for stone and partly from the Arabic word meaning blue. Lapis lazuli is compact, massive, and has a granular texture. It is usually opaque, and its polished surfaces have a waxy luster. Colors range from gray-blue to azure or Berlin-blue. Some pieces display golden flecks of "fool's gold" (pyrite), and these deep blue stones with their pleasing display of pyrite are considered valuable. Its occurrence is rare, which adds to the value. This, combined with the difficulties of working with it, tends to incline the lapidary to use substitutes such as "Swiss lapis" which is a dyed jasper or the material, sodalite. Sodalite is composed of approximately the same minerals but it is formed by intrusive igneous crystallization. In addition, there are paste imitations made of glass or plastic. Although most Chilian lapis is a gray-blue, some stones will display a good medium blue color. Russian lapis tends toward the deeper shades and shows a good display of pyrite. The favorite material of most rockhounds, however—myself included—is from Afghanistan. This material is a vibrant blue, with abundant pyrite. It does not occur in large pieces because it has many internal fractures.

Working with lapis lazuli is challenging and teaches patience. It must be cut slowly, sanded with care to avoid overheating, and polished with tin oxide on a slow leather disc. It almost seems that one must approach this gem with love in order to bring out its hidden beauty. Perhaps this love and patience are necesary in unlocking its mysteries. When I get into lapis, its blue color seems to give me a feeling of peace and harmony. It has a quiet way of encompassing me with universal love and compassion. Perhaps its blue color partly explains this beneficial effect. In the booklet, *Auras,* Edgar Cayce says that blue "has always been the color of the spirit, the symbol of contemplation, prayer, and heaven."

We find clues in the Cayce readings which strongly suggest an interrelationship between the lapis materials:

> In the seeking, as was given in the information, the lapis— not lapis lingua, because that is different but of the same formation, or comes from the same formation—but the lapis is there, in the hall—north side—front of the north window, in the mineral division here [New York Museum of Natural History]—large blue stone. It weighs nearly a ton and has many facets, in the manner in which it was removed from the mines; is from Arizona, and the color necessary for use as instructed—may be seen by stooping below or getting the light through a portion of the upper part, though—to be sure—it's very much thicker than would be necessary for use. It's there! Not lapis linguis, but *lapis!*   440-9

In this reading, we learn several things about lapis: it is blue; it is translucent; it is of the same formation as lapis lingua (notice also the spelling of lingua and linguis); and it comes from Arizona. This reading uses the word lapis, however, not lapis lazuli.

A letter written by Edgar Cayce to [813] describes a relationship that exists between these stones and the persons wearing them.

"Now, about the stone you should wear. I don't know what to say. The reading must have meant something definite when it said blue-green chalcedony. At the next opportunity, where we have a reading in which it would be permissible, we will ask just what this is and where it may be obtained, and under what name. Your experience with this reminds me of that of a young man whose reading told him to wear about his person a lapis linguis. We had never heard of such a stone, and neither had the jeweler; but I was with him several months later when we found one in a mine several hundred feet under the ground (which was being operated for other purposes) out in Arizona. It was of the family of lapis lazuli. So, I hope we will be able to help you find your stone—and not with such great trouble either."
8/2/35 [See 440 series]

This seems to make it clear that lapis lazuli is related to lapis lingua (notice the spelling), that it is from Arizona, and that it was found several hundred feet under ground.

Q-8. Please give my . . . stone . . .
A-8. The lapis lazuli, worn close to the body would be well for the general health of the body—and this you will have to be careful of very soon. The lapis lazuli, of course, is an erosion of copper; but this encased in a glass and worn about the body would be well. 3416-1

Q-5. Where may I find the stone lapis lazuli or lapis ligurius?
A-5. This is an exuding of copper. Either in the copper mines of the southwest, or about Superior, or in Montana. 1931-3

The lapis lazuli stone would be well to wear about the body. This is as chrysalis, to be sure, of copper . . . 880-2

Q-1. Describe in more detail the lapis stone suggested for the body to wear.
A-1. As understood, and may be found by the investigating of same, there is a blue-green stone, that is a fusion in copper deposits, that has the same vibration as the body; and thus is a helpful influence, not merely as an omen or good luck charm, but as the vibratory helpful force for health, for strength, for the ability through the mental self to act upon things, conditions, decisions, and activities.
Because of its softness, it will necessarily have to be encased in glass—as two crystals and this between same. It may be worn around the neck, the wrist or the like. But wear it, for it

will bring health and hope and—best of all—the ability to *do* that so desired. 1651-2

The lapis lazuli, or the rays from copper. 1861-16

Lapis langis, lapis lazuli. This as we find might be said to be a part of the same composition referred to... 1931-2

This may be—will be—a very interesting experiment for the body. Go to the New York Museum of Natural History. Sit by a large quantity of this type of stone and listen at it sing! Do it in the open! Don't let others make a fool of you, or their remarks overcome you—but sit by it and listen at it sing; for it does! It's from Arizona. 440-3

Q-6. This stone contains malachite and azurite. Is the lapis linguis either of these?
A-6. The azurite ...
Q-8. How will I know when I have found this stone that is most useful for my purposes?
A-8. When there is found that [specimen] which is sufficently clear for the transmission of light and that which may be held in the hand for five to ten minutes and then set aside and listening hear the movements or the vibrations given off from the emanations from self. 440-11

Many more quotes could be given, but I think we have sufficient information to draw together a word picture of the lapis lazuli referred to in the readings:

1. Its composition is of copper, either through erosion, fusion, or exuding.
2. Its color is blue or blue-green.
3. It is composed of lapis linguis, and lapis ligurius or part of the same formation.
4. It is soft.
5. It is translucent to transparent.
6. It sings.
7. It is like a chrysalis.

Chrysalis, in this context, has an unusual meaning, and finding it was connected with a special interest of mine. When I have time, I enjoy working with silver and, when I can afford it, gold. There is a technique for achieving a decorative effect on the surface of a stone by applying small spheres to it without using solder. This process is called granulation. The Greeks and the Phoenicians had developed this art to a high degree but, later, the art was lost, and it has only recently been rediscovered. Some years ago, I read a book on metal work in which the author reported on an old manuscript which describes the granulation process. The trick, it seems, is to get those little balls to stay put until molecular fusing takes place. At any rate, one of the adhesives used to accomplish that was called chrysalis. The dictionary defines chrysalis as (among other things): a stage of development or change; golden sheath. Chrysos is from Greek and means gold. In *Popular Gemology*, R.M. Pearl says that chrysocolla is derived from two Greek words and means gold glue. In *Creative Gold and Silversmithing* by S. Choate, copper carbonate is given as one of its ingredients.

The April 1973 issue of the *Lapidary Journal* has an article, "Arizona Minerals in Retrospect," which states that the American Museum of Natural History has "a huge block of azurite ore which is about four feet in each of six directions, and is riddled with vugs lined with botryoidal and crystallized azurite." This description was included along with those of other materials from the Bisbee mining area. However, no mention was actually made as to origin of this particular specimen.

In reading 440-11, lapis linguis is identified as being azurite, and the stone as lapis. Mary Ann Woodward says the stone is copper ore, probably chrysocolla. Fay Clark, author of *Beyond the Light* and the final chapter of *Healing Stones,* says the stone at the museum is chrysocolla. However, he has identified lapis lazuli as being the aluminum material, or as what we know today as lapis lazuli. Rather than attempting to build the case on supposition, it may prove helpful to look at another part of reading 440-11:

Many various characters of this lapis may be found in Arizona, as may be of other stones in the same vicinity of a semi-precious value or nature, but those that are of the greater value as the touchstones or those that may receive (we are putting it in another form or manner) a blessing and transmit same to another, or a curse and transmit same to another, will be found in the nature where the greater portion of the azurite is evidenced in the immediate vicinity.   440-11

Many various characters of this lapis, the reading says, may be found in Arizona. Perhaps a look at some of these variations will shed more light.

Azurite, a basic carbonate of copper, is azure blue in color, opaque to translucent, and in its pure form is too soft (or too brittle) to cut into gems. It is a useful ore of copper. Under normal conditions, it slowly alters to malachite. When both minerals are found together, the resulting stone is called azurmalachite. (*Popular Gemology,* p. 171)

Shattakite is a massive opaque silicifed form of azurite and malachite. In very thin sections, it is translucent. This material will cut into very beautiful gems and, because of its color, is usually set in silver.

Burnite is another gem-grade form of azurite and malachite which comes from Montana. It is an ore of copper, is massive and opaque, will cut, but will not polish well. Its background material is grayish-green. The mine from which it once came is now closed, and no more burnite is available.

Chrysocolla, a translucent hydrous copper silicate with variable composition, is a finely crystalline-like chalcedony quartz. It is colored by delicate hues of green and blue, and possesses a luster which may be either vitreous in quality or enamel-like. This form is more commonly referred to as "electric blue chrysocolla." Found in the upper zone of copper deposits, it is formed by the alteration of primary minerals and is associated with two other gems, azurite and malachite. It is a rarer form of copper ore. (*Popular Gemology,* p. 193) This name, which means "gold glue," was possibly given it by ancient jewelers who may have used it to solder gold.

The chrysocolla of the Bisbee area is more opaque, with veins of clear chalcedony. It is a deep blue-green, and, today, is being sold as "turquoise." This form of chrysocolla, while not as pure as the silica gem form, is the material I am more familiar with. It cuts into very lovely gems, but due to the varying hardness of its component minerals, will show some undercutting. One must be very careful when buying rough chrysocolla. Much of it is so soft and brittle it will not hang together long enough to get a piece cut. Some suppliers are coating this specimen quality with epoxy resin, giving it something of a crystal effect.

"Reflections of a Rockhound" (*The A.R.E. Journal,* Nov. 1973) mentioned my personal sensitivity to copper. As a cutter, I can really get "stoned" on chrysocolla, azurite and malachite. The latter, however, sometimes contains arsenic, and I suggest wearing a dust mask to help keep such poisons out of your lungs! Generally chrysocolla affects me in a variety of ways. Sometimes touching it with my right hand produces a very mild "electrical" shock. At other times this sensation occurs after I lay the stone down. Not all chrysocolla, though, is "hot," and sometimes I feel nothing at all. I suspect this has something to do with mind or, perhaps, body chemistry. In the cutting, when I get into the stone I become aware of a copper taste under my tongue. It seems to give me a feeling of harmony. At the same time, however, it is a very energizing positive feeling. It is a feeling which is very hard to describe—like a drawing in, a sort of attracting essence to myself. With azurite there is the copper taste, the feeling of universal harmony, but there is also a very keen awareness of my surroundings. It even becomes difficult to concentrate on the cutting. It's like an expansion of consciousness. Malachite is one material I have not done much with since my rather bad experience with the arsenic. It produced a burning feeling in my nose and I began having difficulty with breathing. I've passed along the warning about malachite to a lot of rockhounds, and except for one other person who was hospitalized, no one has ever reported any problems.

There is another effect that must be mentioned here—the "singing." In the middle fifties, I had about 150 pounds of "good" to "fine" Bisbee chrysocolla, but all that remains of it are the fond memories of a very fine gem material. Among the memories is my only experience with the "singing." On the 3rd of December, 1973, while I watered my turquoise (turquoise is a hydrous compound of copper and aluminum and loses color when it loses water), I became aware of a very clear, high-pitched chirping, or beeping sound. I thought I was experiencing the sound aurally and that is was brought about by a dehydrated material absorbing water. Thinking it would be of interest to others who had experienced ringing or singing stones, I attempted to tape the sound. On play back, all I could hear was a lot of background sound and the ticking of my watch. What I heard seemed definitely "outside" because the sound decreased as I moved away from the stone. However, if you have ever experienced a person's voice speaking your name when the person was not there—well, you know it sounds like it comes through your ears. But nobody else there hears it! To this day I can't tell you if the ringing of the chrysocolla occurred inside or outside of my head.

Readings dealing with Lapis Lazuli:		Readings referring to Lapis:
691-1	1931-3	440-3
691-2	2072-10	440-9
1651-2	2132-1	440-11
880-2	2282-1	440-12
1532-1	2376-1	440-18
1861-16	2564-3	813-1 (letter)
1981-1	3053-3	816-3
1931-1	3416-1	1580-1
1931-2		1931-4 (letter)

A.R.E. PRESS

The A.R.E. Press publishes quality books, videos, and audiotapes meant to improve the quality of our readers' lives—personally, professionally, and spiritually. We hope our products support your endeavors to realize your career potential, to enhance your relationships, to improve your health, and to encourage you to make the changes necessary to live a loving, joyful, and fulfilling life.

For more information or to receive a free catalog, call

1-800-723-1112

Or write

A.R.E. Press
215 67th Street
Virginia Beach, VA 23451-2061

DISCOVER HOW THE EDGAR CAYCE MATERIAL CAN HELP YOU!

The Association for Research and Enlightenment, Inc. (A.R.E.®), was founded in 1931 by Edgar Cayce. Its international headquarters are in Virginia Beach, Virginia, where thousands of visitors come year round. Many more are helped and inspired by A.R.E.'s local activities in their own hometowns or by contact via mail (and now the Internet!) with A.R.E. headquarters.

People from all walks of life, all around the world, have discovered meaningful and life-transforming insights in the A.R.E. programs and materials, which focus on such areas as holistic health, dreams, family life, finding your best vocation, reincarnation, ESP, meditation, personal spirituality, and soul growth in small-group settings. Call us today on our toll-free number:

1-800-333-4499
or
Explore our electronic visitor's center on the
INTERNET: http://www.are-cayce.com

We'll be happy to tell you more about how the work of the A.R.E. can help you!

A.R.E.
215 67th Street
Virginia Beach, VA 23451-2061